CLIMB YOUR Ladder *of* SUCCESS WITHOUT RUNNING OUT *of* GAS!

*The Simple Truth on H_____
and Ignite Your Ene_____ ____ __ ___ _____ Success*

JOHN M. ROWLEY

MORGAN JAMES PUBLSHING • NEW YORK

CLIMB YOUR Ladder of SUCCESS WITHOUT RUNNING OUT of GAS!

ISBN: 978-1-60037-240-7 (Hardcover)
ISBN: 978-1-60037-239-1 (Paperback)

Part of the MEGABOOK SERIES
Published by:

MORGAN · JAMES
THE ENTREPRENEURIAL PUBLISHER ™
www.morganjamespublishing.com

Morgan James Publishing, LLC
1225 Franklin Ave Ste 32
Garden City, NY 11530-1693
Toll Free 800-485-4943
www.MorganJamesPublishing.com

Cover/Interior Design by:
Rachel Campbell
rachel@r2cdesign.com

Cover Photograph by:
Bud Moffett

Habitat
for Humanity®
Peninsula
Building Partner

DEDICATION

THIS BOOK IS DEDICATED TO the person who held my ladder of success while I was climbing it, even though at times she had to hold the ladder with one hand, while she held our kids with the other. The person who challenged me to think through my goals to make sure my ladder was against the correct wall. To the person who carried my ladder of success, when I was too weary to go on. She encouraged me to take one more rung when I didn't think I had it in me. The person who walked through fire with me, when my ladder fell over and we had to begin over again and again. The person who ran our company, while I put all my energies into this book over the past three or more years ... and then found the time to edit it.

Without this person, this book would not have been possible. Without this person, my life would not have been as successful, fun or full of joy. The person I love the most in this world and the person God chose to bless me with, the mother of my incredible children Jim, John, Jessica and Jacqueline, the mother in-law to my beautiful daughter Jocelyn and the grandmother (Grannae, she feels too young to be a grandma) to our new granddaughter Jennifer Alexis Lynn Rowley "Jenna". My wife and best friend, Cathy. The greatest success I have ever achieved was by getting you to say "Yes! I will marry you". I love you, Cath. Thank you for always being there for me! The ride isn't over yet so fasten your seat belt!

PRAISE FOR
Climb YOUR Ladder of Success
Without Running Out of Gas!

"I HAVE KNOWN JOHN FOR many years and have watched his start from humble beginnings as well as his climb up his own ladder of success. I'm glad he's inspiring you to climb yours!"

BARBARA CORCORAN
AUTHOR, SPEAKER, ENTREPRENEUR

Founder of The Corcoran Group Real Estate in New York City
Author of If You Don't Have Big Breasts, Put Ribbons on Your Pigtails, *an unlikely business book that has become a national best-seller!*

"This book is a treasure trove of nurturing ideas that demonstrate the meaningful journey to success. With the proper balance of a healthy lifestyle and focused mindset, one's dreams are attainable through persistence and careful planning. This inspiring success story is perfect for all ages!"

NIDO QUBEIN
PRESIDENT, HIGH POINT UNIVERSITY

Speaker and Author
Chairman, Great Harvest Bread Co.

"Whether becoming the world's first super model or starting my own modeling agency and T.V. show, failure isn't an option. Energy, passion and an undying will makes things happen. Read this book!"

JANICE DICKINSON
MODEL, AUTHOR, CELEBRITY

Executive Producer, The Janice Dickinson Modeling Agency

"Energy, passion and persistence are necessary ingredients for success. It doesn't matter if you are going for an Olympic Gold, building a business or climbing the corporate ladder, we all need the fuel to turn our dreams into reality. With this book, John shows you how to make it happen."

MITCH GAYLORD
1984 OLYMPIC GOLD MEDALIST

First American Gymnast in history to score a Perfect "10"

"John and I went to the same high school but during different years. We were both under the tutelage of Coach Jim Fraley. Persistence, determination and drive were expected and he drilled that into John and me. As an Olympian, businessman and artist I understand that energy and a positive self attitude are critical. John has reached for the gold with *"Climb YOUR Ladder of Success without Running out of Gas!"* I am pleased to see that he is encouraging others to go for the gold in life as well."

AL OERTER

FOUR TIME OLYMPIAN AND ARTIST

"The keys to success are universal. I have successfully used the same success principles building my custom home building business as I did playing in the NFL. Energy, passion and a desire to succeed are a winning combination. John is a friend and a business associate and I am glad to see he has scored a touch down with this book."

KEN HUFF

BALTIMORE COLTS 1975 – 1982
WASHINGTON REDSKINS 1982 – 1985
OWNER KEN HUFF BUILDERS DURHAM NC

"Being fit and being successful are not opposing goals. In fact, they are complementary of one another. You need an extraordinary amount of energy and discipline to be successful and you nurture both of those while in the gym training. John's principles are simple, but the results you'll achieve will be extraordinary. This book will impact your life forever."

KIRK GALIANI

FORMER CEO/PRESIDENT GOLD'S GYM INTERNATIONAL

Major shareholder of Gold's Gym INT.
Owner of Gold's Gyms in MD, VA, WVA & NC

"As a contributor to my magazine, *Sharing Ideas*, I know first hand that John lives what he is teaching. *Climb YOUR Ladder of Success without Running out of Gas* is a great blueprint for anyone looking for lasting success in life. Read it and more importantly implement it!"

DOTTIE WALTERS
WALTERS SPEAKERS BUREAU

Founding member of the National Association of Speakers
Editor and Publisher of Sharing Ideas *Magazine*

"There is a winner inside each and every one of us. John Rowley in his new book, *"Climb YOUR ladder of Success Without Running Out of Gas"*, shows you how to energize your most important asset...YOU. This book will provide the energy and insights to bring the WINNER out in anyone who reads it."

DR. ERIC SCOTT KAPLAN
BEST SELLING AUTHOR "DR. KAPLAN'S LIFESTYLE OF
THE FIT & FAMOUS." *AND* "DYING TO BE YOUNG,
FROM BOTOX TO BOTULISM"

"Striving for success is one thing, having the energy to actually sustain your efforts over a long enough period of time until you are successful is quite another. John shows you how to make it over the long haul and not only achieve success but to enjoy it and keep it! A must read for anyone striving for success. Get it, read it, do it!"

RICK FRISHMAN
PRESIDENT PLANNED TV ARTS

www.plannedtvarts.com
www.rickfrishman.com

"For decades I have been teaching America's top producing real estate agents how to pursue their real estate business with passion while balancing it with a fulfilling personal life. John is one of those students and I am always so proud when a student takes the information I teach and runs with it. In this book John shows you how to LIVE an energetic, passion filled life... the life of your dreams."

HOWARD J. BRINTON
STAR POWER SYSTEMS

"As a contributor to Iron Man magazine, John has always encouraged our readers to be passionate about bodybuilding and about life. This book obviously comes out of John's zest for the pursuit of excellence. Read this book!"

STEVE HOLMAN
EDITOR IN CHIEF

Iron Man Magazine

"John and I met on an old cinder track in high school and have been close friends for the past thirty years. As high school and college athletes, we know the type of dedication it takes to compete on a high level and the difficulty of training while injured. I have literally seen John reach the pinnacle of success and dive to the depths of despair...without giving up! He took life's best shots, got up, dusted himself off and kept on running. This book is an inspiration and will challenge you to succeed in all areas of your life, no matter what!"

BRIAN MCLAUGHLIN
PRESIDENT OF THE SECURECOM GROUP, LTD.

"Pursuing success with passion is the key to all achievement. Let John energize you and motivate you to a more balanced and healthy lifestyle."

SHERRY GRANADER
NUTRITIONIST, NATIONAL SPEAKER, NATIONALLY CERTIFIED GROUP EXERCISE
INSTRUCTOR, AUTHOR, WRITER, TV AND RADIO HOST

www.sgfit.com

"John worked for our company while working as a janitor in Harlem. Not quite our usual hire but then again, John is unusual. He came in with energy, passion and worked. Period! He got the job done and saddled up to some of our best people so he could learn from them. He was fun to be around and I am proud to call him my friend."

ELAINE DEAN
SENIOR MANAGING DIRECTOR

Corcoran Group Real Estate

"John elevates the principles of success into an incredibly productive art form! Success of any type in life requires tremendous energy, let John energize and inspire you to outstanding success!"

CATHY RUSSELL, CRB, CRS, GRI
CATHY RUSSELL TEAM REAL ESTATE

"I have known John my whole life. As a friend and family member I can tell you that he is living proof that energy and the determination to succeed works! As a doctor I can testify that keeping your body in tip top shape makes climbing your ladder of success much easier and more enjoyable."

MARK A. ROWLEY MD

"I knew John when he was still green in Manhattan Real Estate. That didn't last long. John was one of the most dynamic real estate people that I have ever met and he combined this with a very warm, friendly demeanor. I am proud to call John my friend. Read this book, John brings a new meaning to success!"

LOU ROMANO
EXECUTIVE VICE PRESIDENT

Stuyvesant Fuel Service

"John opens the doors to a successful life with this inspiring book. I have worked with John and have been close friends for almost two decades. He brings his passion to work, to the gym and home. I am proud he is my friend and pleased he is bringing his proven principles of success to others."

MITCH MAYER
FORMER DIRECTOR OF MANAGEMENT

Sultzberger-Rolfe Real Estate N.Y., N.Y

"I have worked with John personally on my own fitness program and can attest to his knowledgeable and entertaining approach to mental and physical fitness. His energy is infectious."

SCOTT FAIRBROTHER **MD**

"I have known John since he was a high school athlete. I followed John's path with a keen interest. John has always attacked his goals and ambitions; often taking chances that would have made the average man sick. I always said tongue in cheek, that he would either be an incredible success or be homeless. I am glad John is not homeless, and that he is willing to share the many lessons he has learned on his way to success. It is an incredible journey of blood sweat and tears and good old fashion muscle that will inspire all who read his story."

GREGORY F. MCLAUGHLIN

ACKNOWLEDGEMENTS

THIS BOOK, LIKE EVERYTHING ELSE in my life, is the result of the help of many. I extend my deepest and most heartfelt thanks to:

Rick Frishman, the man who jump-started my publishing efforts after nearly four years of researching, writing, rewriting, working with a literary agent, having that literary agent go AWOL never to be heard from again and simply banging my head against the wall. Rick listened to me on the phone, fielded all my emails and guided me so artfully into the hands of an incredible publisher that I got more accomplished with Rick's guidance in a few months than I did all those years by myself. Also the guidance and exposure you are helping me to get are a dream come true. Rick, you are truly incredible!

Mark Victor Hanson, your advice took me from simply thinking about writing a book to being a published author. Your story has not only encouraged me, but inspired me. The way you have fun, while helping others to be their best is incredible. Without you I never would have met Rick Frishman. Thank you for paving the way..

David Hancock, the man who not only published this book but believed in me and caught the vision for this project. I look forward to many years of working together. Thank you for believing in me and for being a good friend.

Laurie Majors, my counselor. You guided me when I had no idea what to do. You opened my eyes to an industry I knew nothing about. You rejoiced with me during my victories and prayed and encouraged me during my struggles. Thank you for being there for me. Thank you for believing in me.

Barbara Corcoran, you opened my eyes to a new world. You told me that I would never be happy working for anyone else that I would always work for myself. In fact, you tried to help me with that during the time we were looking at buying different property management companies. You introduced me to a new world of possibilities. When I did go out on my own, you sent a gift to my new business and encouraged me. When I closed that business, you told me that we all have setbacks and you gave me a job and spurred me on. When it was time for me to move on, you encouraged me. Thank you for always being in my corner and for being a good friend and mentor.

Bruce Barbour. For giving me direction and guidance when I had none. You breathed life to the early words of this book and that life stayed through all of the chapters. Thank you for your help and guidance.

Jim Anthony for taking the time to make sure that my ladder was leaning against the correct wall and for taking the time to mentor me through my faith in Christ.

Chris Mangum, for standing with me in prayer during the good times and the bad, God has truly blessed me through our relationship.

Brian McLaughlin. You lived much of my life's story with me. You are the lifelong friend that stood with me when I was at the heights of exhilaration and helped me up when I plummeted to the ground. You always had faith in me and encouraged me to be my best. You also didn't hesitate to correct me when I was wrong. That is the mantle of a true friend.

Mitch Mayer. You endured endless conversations about this book and encouraged me every step of the way. You read the unreadable manuscript and told me it was great. Every time there was a set back and I kept going you told me that *"this is how it happens, the successful go on when others quit."* We started out as the "odd couple" of Madison Avenue and have forged a lifetime friendship that endures the test of time, a friendship that is truly priceless.

John Guelzow for not only encouraging me but for giving me the much needed cardio equipment that I use daily.

Andrew Lyons. Even though you were busy climbing your own ladder of success, you visited me often while I was bed ridden after my accident. You were there for me when I needed you.

Richard Kolarov for setting an example of excellence in the work place and for standing with me as a good friend as I struggled through this book.

Pastor Chad Harvey, for standing boldly on the word of God and for standing with me in prayer while encouraging me to fulfill Gods call on my life.

Ross Paterson. My friend, mentor and most of all a chap that is always there for me. Even though you speak funny, you always have the words to touch and transform my life. You are a hero to many and I am proud to call you my friend.

Jim Fraley. You had the team carry me to the track so I would join your team and not go to another high school. The thanks I got for going with you was in how you encouraged me, beat me up, pushed me beyond my limits, had me train two and sometime three times per day, many times in the rain and snow, had me train and compete during the summer when everyone else was having fun. You gave me the ability to face failure head on and to work harder than anyone else so it wouldn't happen again. You believed in me and by you believing in me, you made me believe in myself. I watched you candidly help the less fortunate students with your own money and encourage them to be their best. You are one of the best things that could have happened to me. You may be gone but you aren't' forgotten. You had an impact that endures. Because of you, my life is better.

Serrell Read who read the manuscript and provided much needed feedback and editing.

To the following people who directly influenced my thinking about success and living a balanced life over the years, some through personal relationship and others through their books, seminars and tapes. Jack Canfield, Zig Ziglar, Dottie Walters, Nido Qubein, Arnold Schwarzenegger, Sylvester Stallone, Harvey Mackay, Al Oerter, Donald Trump, Harry Helmsley, Leona Helmsley, Mark Harris, Florio Roettger, John Maxwell, Lou Ferrigno, Larry Scott, Bill Pearle, Bill Kazmaier, Howard Briton, Joe Weider, Steve Weinberger, Bev Francis, Ray "Thunder" Stern, Elaine Dean, Jeff Levitas, Dan Douglas, Ken Huff, Pat Teague, Jim Sink, and Danny Lotz. This is the short list. I have had so many people help me over the years that I simply can't think of everyone but you know who you are.

To my parents, Jim and AnnMarie Rowley. Thank you for the sacrifices you made over the years so that me and my brothers Mark and James could have more in life. You set an example of integrity that I try to live by daily.

And finally to my children, Jim, John, Jessica and Jacqueline. The most significant success I have or will ever have is the joy of watching you grow into incredible young men and women. I am very proud of you all! If I would have known what true success was, I would have been home with you and Mom more during the early years instead of pursuing the illusion of success. I gave up much by not being there with you more. I have learned so much from you. Jim your caring, John your patience, Jessie your diligence and Jacqui your joy and from all of you, the love that transcends the mistakes a father makes. I am also excited by the way the Lord is blessing our family with its newest members. My new daughter, Jocelyn and my new granddaughter Jennifer Alexis-Lynn Rowley "Jenna". If I would have known how much fun it was to be a father in law and a grandfather, I would have been so much nicer to your husband and father, my son John. You all and your mother are the greatest gift God could have bestowed on me.

TABLE OF CONTENTS

FOREWORD

PASSION, PERSISTENCE AND AN UNWAVERING determination to succeed are all essential ingredients of success. All of these incredible attributes of success are useless if you don't have the energy to implement them.

I am so pleased that John is putting the energy into helping others succeed in life. Even though John has encountered many road blocks climbing his own ladder of success he never let his enthusiasm die. John's passion and enthusiasm for life is infectious and that comes through in the pages to follow.

I know first hand that energy and passion are necessary for success in life. Whether it be trying to get *"Chicken Soup for the Soul"* published, building a speaking career, growing a business or going around the world encouraging others to be the best they can be, it takes strength, energy and passion to not only peruse but to realize your dreams.

I am glad to see that John is encouraging you to challenge your body, mind and spirit so you can climb your own personal ladder of success, what ever it may be. Success requires not only starting strong but finishing strong. I know he is the right man for the job and I am proud to see one of my student's help you pursue your dreams.

Read this book but more importantly implement this book!

Good luck on your own personal journey

MARK VICTOR HANSEN
AUTHOR OF "CHICKEN SOUP FOR THE SOUL"
AND "THE ONE MINUTE MILLIONAIRE"

America's Ambassador of Possibility

INTRODUCTION

The Success Factor!

IF THERE IS ONE INGREDIENT that sets the successful apart from the rest, I would have to say it would be their passion. The dictionary says that passion is *a strong liking or desire for, or devotion to some activity, object, or concept.* One thing I have noticed over the years is that anyone that I have known or met that was successful had a passion. It didn't matter if they were successful in sports, business, non-profit endeavors, family life or any other area. If they were successful, they had an unwavering passion.

On January 3, 2007 Oprah Winfrey had a show called *"What class are you? Inside America's taboo topic."* I thought it was handled in a wonderful and very well balanced way. In fact, I loved the way Oprah stood her ground, as she disagreed with the "luck equation" to success and said that *luck happens when preparation meets opportunity!*

One thing did get my goat though. One of the guests said that it is harder to get ahead today than ever before. Tell that to my grandparents and countless others who lost everything during the depression. My grandparents went from a beautiful home on Long Island to a two bedroom apartment, over a shoe store in Brooklyn, where they raised six very successful and productive children.

Oprah's guest also said that the ladder of success is so much longer today and that it is almost impossible to climb. My burning question is this *"Is the ladder longer? Or are we just weaker and more tired as a society?"* He stated that twenty and thirty years ago it was easier to climb that ladder than now. I say the problem is the obesity and lack of energy in America that has turned into an epidemic over that same time period. So is the ladder longer or are we just finding it harder to climb because we are physically, emotionally and spiritually exhausted? I agree with Oprah, opportunity is still alive and well in America today. You need to prepare for it and work toward your goals. All of which takes, energy, patience, persistence, determination and most importantly passion. And never, ever let anyone else dictate your future, even the experts that write books or end up on talk shows. They are just telling you that they know THEY can't do it!

It is passion that gets us out of bed in the morning before the alarm. It is passion that keeps that spring in our step. It is passion that pushes us when others quit. It is passion that others notice when speaking to you. Passion comes through to others. In fact, it will inspire others. Adlai Stevenson said of Cicero, *"When Cicero spoke, the people stood and cheered. When Demosthenes spoke, the people stood and marched!"* I wasn't there when Demosthenes spoke over 2,000 years ago, but I bet he spoke with passion, a passion that inspired the people of his day to march and not just cheer.

When you read this book I want you to march. I want to meet you one day at a seminar or at an airport and have you tell me that you read my book and got up and got going! You took control of your life with the principles in this book and made your life better for you, your family and your world. You didn't just read this book…you used it! That is my passion.

Passion and enthusiasm are transferable but so is a yawn. I want to transfer my passion for living life to its fullest to you. When you experience the results of living a healthy and vibrant lifestyle your passion will flow over to your family and friends. Anthony Robbins says that success leaves clues and it does. Success also requires energy. _You_ are part of everything you do. If _you_ don't have the energy to pursue success, _you_ will run out of gas while climbing your ladder of success. When someone is yawning look away, but when someone is excelling take notes. Hey I like that! That is worth repeating. *When someone is yawning look away, but when someone is excelling take notes.* In other words, model the successful people and you will get similar results.

My Passion

For more than a quarter of a century, I have been studying the principles of success and physical fitness from the gym rat's point of view and also from the perspective of a business owner, corporate executive, church member and concerned family member. In the process, I have come to realize that both passion and physical fitness are necessary for success and actually work together…not separately. I initially studied the two as different, but interesting disciplines because I was interested in both. Along the way I have made some very important distinctions on how they tie together. In fact, they support each other. The importance of our physical health is undeniable, and to achieve the things we want in our lives we need the energy and focus that comes from a healthy lifestyle.

This book is called *"Climb YOUR Ladder of Success Without Running Out of Gas!"* because I truly believe that your fitness and energy levels influence every area of your life, just as the lack of energy, vibrancy and strength permeates all areas of your life.

This book is going to show you how to prepare yourself for success from the inside out. I will show you how to:

1. Turn energy leaks into dynamic energy which is the fuel of success.
2. Fuel your body for spectacular health and energy.
3. Dramatically transform your body into a muscle building, fat burning dynamo.
4. Unleash your passion, purpose and drive.
5. Master the power of a positive mind-set with ever increasing faith.
6. Harness the physiology of success. Emotion is created by motion!
7. Use the success of others to remodel yourself.
8. And much more!

Once you have these things going for you, you will be able to take what you learn in this book with regards to goal setting and time management and apply them to other areas of your life. Then because you have more energy, feel better and are more confident in how you look & present yourself, you can go out and conquer your world. Finally, out of your passion you will show others how to do it. I know you will have successes building on top of themselves until you are the person you were created to be. The world needs your gifts and talents. It is your responsibility to bring yourself to the world.

I am going to show you what works without the fluff. I will share with you the way it really is, instead of giving you vague theories and techniques. This will help you to avoid all the years of study, trial and error that I went through. You can simply put your time and energy to do the things that work. *The world rewards us for what we do, not for what we know or have.* Now let's dig in and start doing the things that will give you the life of our dreams.

CHAPTER

$$\boxed{1}$$

Creating Optimum Balance

"Just as your car runs more smoothly and requires less energy to go faster and farther when the wheels are in perfect alignment, you perform better when your thoughts, feelings, emotions, goals, and values are in balance." —BRIAN TRACY

I WROTE THIS BOOK FOR ME!

Thanks for joining me while I write to myself. When I first began writing this book, I wrote it to get myself going again. I knew what to do. I had all the tools, but I wasn't using them effectively. Before I knew it, I was 30 lbs. over weight, exhausted and didn't even realize it. Eventually, I decided I would write a fitness and diet plan for myself. I'd read all the books, been to all the seminars and had a great background in this area. Once I started writing, I realized

1

that other people would benefit from my journey, so my notes turned into the book you are reading. The amazing thing to me is how this has turned into a life plan. Every area of my life affects my energy and health. It's not limited to just my diet and exercise program. I hope my journey helps you to develop your life plan as much as it has helped me.

A WAKE UP CALL

One day I walked into my kitchen and there on the refrigerator was a cartoon picture of a middle aged guy in boxers with one sock on and one sock off, over weight and bald. He was looking into the mirror and what he saw was a muscular, vibrant, handsome, young man with a full head of hair. He was standing there in his bathing suit flexing his incredibly muscular body. I thought it was absolutely hysterical ....until I realized my wife had put it up there to get my attention.

Yikes, that was me! Yes, I still lifted weights and had muscle but I'd let my diet go. I didn't move very much. Running, biking or any type of cardio vascular exercise was non-existent. Even though I had muscle I was fat, tired, depressed and getting nowhere fast. I was taking a nap whenever I could and I didn't have the energy to do anything that I didn't have to do. I was standing in front of the mirror and looking back at me was a vague memory, not reality…I was fooling myself. Fortunately, I didn't fool my wife and she loved me enough to prod me into action. She knew I didn't want to live the way I was living and she was willing to do something about it.

Writing this book has helped me in a few important ways. First, it made me realize that my energy leaks didn't just come from being overweight. In fact, being overweight happened because I had energy leaks. I not only had leaks in my body, but also in my mind and spirit. In other words, I found out that taking care of my body with diet and exercise was simply not enough. I needed to have a healthy mental attitude and a sound spiritual life. This would plug my energy leaks. For example, I could be in great physical shape but if I was worrying all of the time, my energy would still be zapped. So I came to the conclusion that I didn't just need a new diet or exercise plan. I needed to work on all of me! This book has evolved into a complete life's plan addressing all areas of your life. This book addresses the body, mind and spirit, so you will benefit immediately, completely and long term.

My friend Bruce Barbour prodded me in this direction. He simply asked me a question to ponder, "Has your energy gone up since you started on your spiritual walk, at age 35?" He knew I understood the mental and physical dimension to energy and passion but he was asking if my spiritual life played a role also. My initial response was, "No!" And was I adamant. He then asked me to think about it.

Later that day, I asked my wife that same question and to my surprise she gave me a resounding "YES!" "Are you kidding me?" I indignantly told her, "I had plenty of energy before! In fact, I outworked everyone!" Boy was I put out! "I have always been a very high energy guy", I grumbled. I really didn't want the truth. I just wanted her to tell me what I wanted to hear. Cathy agreed that I had always had high energy, but she also told me, "You used to have only two speeds, hyper and off. Now you have sustainable energy. You still have hyper speed and off, but you also have gears in-between that allow you to be much more effective in life. And quite honestly, you are more fun! More fun because you have the energy to put into us now, not just energy for work." I hated hearing it, but that was the turning point in my personal journey and beginning of this writing of this book.

The bottom line is I am not a fitness model, someone with great genetics or a straight "A" student. I am not the kind of person that everything comes easy to. I am an average guy with common challenges that has had the opportunity to study and pursue my passions. I am now going to share some of what I have learned during my continued pursuit for fitness, my study of the science of success conditioning and my search for a sound spiritual life to help you save many years of trial and error in these areas of your life. Why reinvent the wheel when you can implement what has taken me 30 years to learn? During your own exciting journey, I just hope to be a good coach and friend while pointing you in the right direction.

WHERE ARE YOU RIGHT NOW?

Let's get right to the point. Anything in life worth pursuing will require some investment of energy on your part. Did you know that most people don't fail in life because they lack the ability, the intelligence or the skill? They fail because they run out of emotional, physical and spiritual gas while climbing the ladder of success. _*They simply don't have the energy to succeed.*_ You can have the best education, outstanding skills, be highly intelligent and possess all the ability in the world and still fail! That's right, you can have it all and still fall flat on your face. It happens every day! The reverse is also true, you can be lacking in those attributes and still become a raving success. Don't you know someone like that? They shouldn't be successful but they are? Success lies not in what you have but in what you DO with what you have. ***You must have the energy to fuel your passions, abilities and skills in order to be successful.***

Is lack of energy stopping you from fulfilling your destiny? Are you too tired to do all the things you want to do or worse yet, all the things you need to do? Are you living a life of passion or are you just going through the motions? If you can relate to not having enough "oomph" to get through the day, much less fulfill your destiny, you are not alone.

People from all walks of life are too tired to pursue their destinies. Their spirits may be willing, but their bodies and minds are tired. Success requires energy! *Energy is the fuel to ignite passion and passion is the engine of success!* Everyone is created to operate at peak performance and to pursue their passions, yet lifestyle choices can stop us from really living. Right choices will quickly give you energy to live a life of passion! Isn't that encouraging? All you need to do is change a few things and you can have the life of your dreams.

SUCCESS COMES FROM WHAT YOU DO, NOT FROM WHAT YOU HAVE.

Let me share someone's life history with you. This was a man who:
- At the age of 21 he failed in business.
- At the age of 22 he lost a state legislative race.
- At the age of 24 he failed in business again.
- At the age of 26 his sweetheart died.
- At the age of 27 he had a nervous breakdown.

- At the age of 34 he lost a congressional race.
- At the age of 36 he lost another congressional race.
- At the age of 45 he lost a senatorial race.
- At the age of 47 he lost a race for vice-president.
- At the age of 49 he again lost a senatorial race.
- At the age of 52 he was elected President of the United States.

This man was Abraham Lincoln.

Could he have become President of the United States if he didn't "keep on keeping on"? This man did not give up. He was also very energetic and fit. He kept pushing forward in life until he succeeded. He must have been very passionate about what he was doing. He was willing to put in the required energy to pursue his dreams and to change a nation. I bet old Abe also changed himself in the process. Abe Lincoln is an example in perseverance and determination. He may not have been the smartest, most educated or best looking man of his time but he certainly used what he was given and didn't give up on his dream.

My friend Brian McLaughlin sent this to me to help me keep my spirits up when I was struggling. I kept this timeline of Abe Lincoln's life over my desk for many years to help me persevere through some tough times. I have been one step from being homeless. I have had times when our family didn't have food to eat. We have had our electricity turned off, our water turned off and we have had to give back a car we didn't want to. We have had the sheriff at our door giving us an eviction notice and we have had times when we couldn't afford medical care for our children or ourselves. We had the Revenue Department take every penny we had without notice. I have been put in jail. I have lost more than one business…but I have never, ever given up.

For year's people, especially family, criticized me, laughed at me or were embarrassed by me. They didn't encourage me. They wanted me to give up. Because they couldn't do something I was pursuing, they thought I couldn't do it either. I didn't accept that. Did I have times of despair? You bet! Did I have any doubt that I could make it? Yes! But I knew, without a doubt, that if I gave up that I definitely wouldn't make it. I also knew that if I could overcome failure enough times that I would ultimately prevail.

I had people kicking me when I was down but I was blessed to have the most important person in my life, my wife Cathy, struggle through this with me. She believed in me and told me so. Even in the midst of it all, she believes in me. All this to say, that I feel qualified to encourage you and tell you that no matter where you are today, as long as you "keep on keeping on", you can succeed tomorrow! Invest the energy to get yourself going in the right direction and you will overcome all the odds, no matter how great they seem at this moment. Education or lack there of, isn't the issue. The real issue is, are you willing to do what it takes to get what you want? **Well, are you?** I think you are or you wouldn't be reading this book. I feel we are kindred spirits because I know you may be where I was and I want you to know that you **can** do it! You were created for greatness!

A Tonic for Increased Energy?

Even back in the 1950's, people were starting to see the need for increasing their energy. Lucille Ball was there to help. She may have been the 1st fad TV diet guru. In a memorable episode of <u>I Love Lucy</u>, she manages to get a role as the "Vitameatavegamin Girl" and is tasked with trying to sell the public a tonic that has healthy amounts of vitamins, meat, vegetables, minerals - and a less healthy dose of alcohol. During a number of rehearsals, Lucy has to drink some of the dreadful-tasting tonic. Due to the high alcoholic content, Lucy begins to get drunk and slur her lines. By the time she goes live with the commercial, her lines "Do you poop out at parties? Are you unpopular?" become "Do you pop out at parties? Are you un-poopular?" Then she chugs down the Vitameatavegamin bottle to the roaring laughter of the studio audience. Let's start looking at what the real *"tonic"* for increased energy, health and vitality is!

FUEL YOUR BODY FOR SPECTACULAR HEALTH AND ENERGY.

This book is called *Climb YOUR Ladder of Success Without Running Out of Gas,* because I truly believe that you need energy to be successful in every area of your life. Just as the lack of energy, vibrancy and strength permeates all areas of your life in a negative way, having energy can transform your life into something spectacular. You can have all the tools and ability in the world, but if you don't have the energy to use what you have, you are dead in the water!

You can't drive across the country on half a tank of gas. You would expect your car to stop short of your intended destination, because it didn't have enough fuel to make it. In fact, you wouldn't push your pet to stay up all night, feed it fatty foods and let it smoke cigarettes would you? You certainly wouldn't expect it to be spry and healthy if it did. If you wouldn't treat a pet that way, why do you treat yourself that way? What do you have against yourself? I know you don't do it on purpose, none of us do. But what happens is that our bad decisions stack on top of each other and then one day we wake up and we are not happy with where we are or what we see. Worse yet, we don't know what to do! This book will change all of that for you forever.

A simple lifestyle change in the way you feed your body, exercise and rest will prepare your body for success. It will give you tons of energy and make you look better which will, in turn, fuel your confidence. Diet and exercise don't need to be consuming in order to work. They just need to be consistent. When you are through with this book you will have a simple plan that will dramatically increase your energy and have you looking better and feeling more vibrant. This plan will give you the energy and the confidence to go out and create the life of your dreams and achieve outstanding success in all areas of your life without running out of gas. <u>You will now have the energy to fuel your passion and to live the life you always dreamed of living!</u>

HARNESS THE PHYSIOLOGY OF SUCCESS. EMOTION IS CREATED BY MOTION!

Your body and mind work together to ignite your energy for lifelong success. When your body is energetic, your mind will follow. Unfortunately, the reverse is also true. Fortunately, there are ways that you can supercharge your energy at a moments notice and at will. You will learn how to ignite your energy when it is needed most. You will also get a formula that will instantly increase your energy and passion to transform your life forever! Your emotions will follow your motions, so you can move your body powerfully!

IGNITE YOUR MIND:

Turn energy leaks into passionate energy which is the fuel of success.

"Nothing great in the world has been accomplished without passion" —GEORG WILHELM FRIEDRICH HEGEL

I am passionate about passion because it ignites the mind. Your mind can take a mental energy leak and transform it into *"success fuel"* by simply changing your focus. The dictionary says that passion is "a strong liking or desire for, or devotion to some activity, object, or concept." One thing I have noticed over the years is that anyone I have known or met who was successful had a passion. It didn't matter if they were successful in sports, business, church life, non-profit endeavors, mission work, environmental work, family life or any other area. If they were successful, they had passion for the pursuit.

UNLEASH YOUR PASSION, PURPOSE AND DRIVE.

I had heard about her for years. I had read about her in the New York Times and had heard people sing her praises over lunch at *Sparks* and the *Post House* in Manhattan. I'd also overheard the jealous saying she was lucky, and yet others had said she was the best ever to attack the New York real estate scene. In her own words, her credentials included straight D's in high school and college and over twenty jobs by the time she had turned twenty-three. It was her next job that would make her one of the most successful entrepreneurs in the country—when she borrowed $1,000.00 from her boyfriend and quit her job as a waitress to start a tiny real estate company in New York City. Over the next twenty-five years, she'd parlay that $1,000.00 loan into New York City's leading Real Estate Company with over $5 billion in closed sales volume in 2003, with 45 offices having more than 2,150 sales associates and employees in New York City, the Hamptons and Palm Beach.

Her name is Barbara Corcoran, founder of The Corcoran Group, and I am happy to call her my friend. Barbara is very high energy and her mind never stops because she loves what she does. She is extremely passionate about everything she does and is a trend setter. She constantly pushes the envelope and that keeps her jazzed. She doesn't sit around on her past accomplishments. In fact, she sold The Corcoran Group and then went out and wrote a National Bestseller, _USE WHAT YOU'VE GOT AND OTHER BUSINESS LESSONS I LEARNED FROM MY MOM_, where she reveals her secret to success. According to CNN, Barbara is "the most sought after broker" in the City and is considered one of the most powerful brokers in the country. Not bad for a poor girl from New Jersey. Barbara is one of those people that I look to for inspiration because she is always positive, uplifting and looking toward the future with a gleam in her eye. She loves life and is passionate about what the future has in store. She's always looking for new challenges and ways to improve what she is doing. She keeps her brain engaged all the time and doesn't allow the inevitable "failures" in life get her down. She uses them to push her further UP the ladder of success.

> *"If there is no passion in your life, then have you really lived?*
> *Find your passion, whatever it may be.*
> *Become it, and let it become you and you will find*
> *great things happen FOR you, TO you and BECAUSE of you."*
> **—T. ALAN ARMSTRONG**

Passion is always obvious and not always used for profit. When you combine your life's purpose to your passion you will have an incredible drive to pursue your passion. My friend Danny Lotz runs a local men's Bible study. Danny has been a dentist for years, but also leads an incredible bible study every Friday morning. A group of over 100 men gather in a restaurant of a local hotel to discuss a particular scripture and how it affects their lives. Danny's passion is to make a difference in these men's lives. This passion is what attracts men to this event at 7:00 AM every Friday morning. When other men are just getting ready for work or having their first cup of coffee, these men are implementing the word of God into their lives.

Danny is not jumping up and down and hanging from the rafters to demonstrate his passion. In fact, he is a low-key, very humble man who exudes passion…a quiet, humble passion, but a burning passion for what he is doing. Yes, you can have both. You don't need to change who you are to be a passionate person. Passion is not an outward physical action. It is an inward burn. A burn you just can't shake. A determination no one can talk you out of. You just know, that you know, that you should be doing what you are doing regardless of what others may think. It is part of you and fires up your life.

Having your mind directed toward goals like Barbara Corcoran, or on giving back to the people in your community like, Danny Lotz, will give you a desire that your mind just won't let go of. Passion comes from within, from your thoughts and from what you focus on. You will become what you think about all the time. Direct your thought life in a positive direction and positive things will happen in your life.

MASTER THE POWER OF A POSITIVE MIND-SET WITH EVER INCREASING FAITH.

But those who hope in the LORD will renew their strength. They will soar on wings like eagles; they will run and not grow weary, they will walk and not be faint.
—ISAIAH 40:31

Isn't that incredible news! Energy isn't just mental and physical, although they both play an important role. Having a sound spiritual life will keep your body and mind soaring.

Anger, worry, and fear will all sap your energy really quickly. I have a tendency to be a little hot tempered at times, so I decided to turn to God's Word to see what He had to say on the subject. In Job 5:2 God tells me, *"Resentment kills a fool, and envy slays the simple"*. Heck! I don't want to be a simple fool! Then in Eccl. 7:9 He tells me, *"Do not be quickly provoked in your spirit, for anger resides in the lap of fools."* Again, I am a fool if I get angry. Man! I am from New York and where I come from no one talks to me like that! To tell you the truth, I am getting a little hot under the collar about now. Then He adds insult to injury in Prov. 25:28 by telling me, *"Like a city whose walls are broken down is a man who lacks self-control."* So, basically, if I allow myself to get angry I am a simple fool who is falling apart. You know what? When I get angry that is exactly how I feel! Now, before I ever get angry, these scriptures pop up in my mind and spirit and I chuckle to myself. Hey! I am not going to allow myself to be a simple fool…well not on purpose anyway.

I have always been one to immerse myself in my work. I study it. I tweak it to make it more efficient. I practice it. I do it. Whatever "it" is. When you work hard, it all works out, or so I thought. We'd had some struggle before but after we moved to Raleigh, NC from New York City, we started having severe financial struggles which I thought would never end. Although at the time I was working as hard as I could, it just never seemed to get better. Millard Kirk, a friend and co-worker, gave me Proverbs 22:29 to ponder. It says, *"Do you see a man skilled in his work? He will serve before kings; he will not serve before obscure men."* Boy! Did this excite me. This reminded me that if someone was skilled in their work and continued pushing along, that they would prosper. They would serve among kings. My energy went through the roof and I started working even harder. I also stopped working Sunday's that same year; a big no- no in residential real estate sales. I had faith in myself to do the job in less days and faith that God would honor the time I was taking off to honor Him. That year, I got the coveted *Hustler of the Year Award* from RE/MAX! The bottom line is to continually build your faith by putting good things into your mind so you will feel more confident. Make sure you have affirming people in your life who will give you nuggets of truth to hold on to when you are struggling.

A common question I hear at motivational seminars is, "What would you do if you knew you could not fail?" Well, I want to ask you, "What would you do if you had the faith that you will succeed? If you believe it, you will achieve it!" Don't just hope for it, go for it. Have faith that you will succeed and you will.

USE THE SUCCESS OF OTHERS TO REMODEL YOURSELF.

You don't have to be the best athlete in the world, the sharpest guy in your office, or the shrewdest entrepreneur in town. You just have to know how to find them. Seek out the best and find out what makes them tick. Finding people to model is just a matter of looking for people that are successful in the area you are focusing on. Get curious and find out what they do in this area, and then do what they do and you will get similar results. Next become a person worth modeling and start giving back to others.

You are a gift to the world!

You are here for a reason. The world needs your special gifts. *Your talents are God's gifts to you, what you do with them are God's gift to the world.* The world needs what you have to offer. You'll find that your gifts are directly related to what you are passionate about. Find your passion in life and you will find your purpose in life. It is a gift to the world and the wrapping on that gift looks just like you. You are wonderfully and beautifully created and you are powerful. You can have a powerful race car, but if you don't turn the key, you will never see its power and speed. You are much like that race car. You have to turn yourself on in order to see your potential. You have to ignite your body, mind and spirit and when you do…watch out because you are spectacular and created for greatness.

Let's face it. Pursuing your dreams with passion will require energy on your part. There is no getting around that truth. You don't have to run out of emotional, physical and spiritual gas while climbing the ladder of success. Follow the simple steps in this book and you will run up the ladder of success. When you implement this material you will strengthen your body, mind and spirit. You will have not only the energy for success, but you will have true and lasting success. Remember, success lies in what you do with your skills, abilities and talents. Just possessing skills, abilities and talents do nothing unless you use them. You must also have the energy to fuel your passions in order to be successful.

START RIGHT WHERE YOU ARE

"Don't wait until everything is just right. It will never be perfect. There will always be challenges, obstacles and less than perfect conditions. So what. Get started now. With each step you take, you will grow stronger and stronger, more and more skilled, more and more self-confident and more and more successful."

—MARK VICTOR HANSEN

You probably have much more going for you than I did for me. I was a college athlete with aspiring goals. My life's focus on the track and off, in season and out was geared towards me meeting my goals. Then my career was cut short by a near fatal car accident. My life was shattered along with my body.

My mom and dad were not ones to let you sit around idle. They always wanted you to strive for something. I had no alternate plans in my mind to strive for, so they pushed me to just do anything. My dad knew I needed to be doing something and was willing to help me "get going" again. He got me a job working at a grammar school. That is how I ended up working as a janitor.

In fact, when I started my career as a janitor I couldn't even walk unassisted. After my car accident, my dad had gotten me a special walker so I could get around. I attached the cast on my arm onto it which gave me the stability to walk on the one good leg I had. I was in a ton of pain but I worked with what I had. I couldn't even drive at first, so my dad dropped me off and picked me up from work until I was able to drive again.

The man I worked for once told me, in his heavy Irish brogue, that I out-worked every man that he had. And "you did it all with one arm, one leg and no nose!" (said with an Irish brogue and followed by a hearty laugh). Well, I did have a nose. It was cut off in the accident... but they put it back on. I think his words were generous, but they sure were encouraging.

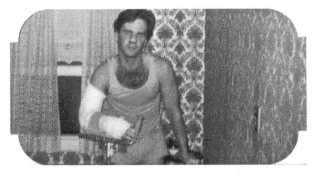

Some years later, I had the nerve to think that a janitor could tackle the high powered world of Manhattan real estate and the dynamic international field of fitness. Once I was successful, they called it "nerve" or "chutzpah" but when I was starting out, they just called me stupid. Many told me I couldn't do it but I thought I could and that was all that mattered. Did I fail? Absolutely! More than most, but I picked myself up, brushed myself off and got going again. I kept my eye on the prize, not on the obstacles and that is a great distinction.

In real estate, I made a name for myself managing some of the most prestigious properties on Park Avenue and the upper east side of New York and managing the holdings for many notables including Harry and Leona Helmsley. I usually took on properties no one else wanted and turned them into properties everyone wanted. Keep in mind this was not a strategy, the only buildings I was given were the ones no one else wanted. I decided I would turn this negative into a positive very quickly.

I was also privileged to own R&J Health Studio, the gym known as "The East Coast Mecca of Bodybuilding." R&J Health Studio received international attention when it was featured in the movie, "Pumping Iron", starring Arnold Schwarzenegger and Lou Ferrigno. I didn't tell you this to impress you. I told you this to *impress upon you* that even though I had humble beginnings, I didn't let that hold me back and neither should you. It doesn't matter where you are starting, the key is to start.

Now let's get to work!

Action Steps

> *Remember, the world doesn't reward us for what we know;*
> *We are rewarded for what we do!*

Below is a place for you to start taking stock of yourself and your life. As you go through the book, we will get deeper into these and other areas. But this will help you to put together a short term action plan so you can start seeing results today.

1. Take an honest look at yourself and see where you need improvement. Should you put a picture on the refrigerator like my wife did for me?

2. Write a list of the areas you must work on to improve, so you can live the life of your dreams. Look at all areas, your body, mind and spirit.

3. Write a list of the things you are passionate about. What would you love to do every day, even if you didn't get paid to do it?

4. Use positive self talk and watch your life turn around.

5. Find someone who is successful in the areas you want to excel in and find out what that person does.

2

Persistence and Determination: The Seeds of Passion

"Success is almost totally dependent upon drive and persistence.
The extra energy required to make another effort or try another approach is the secret
of winning."—**DENNIS WAITLEY**

Living the life of your dreams doesn't happen by accident. It takes deliberate daily action and the ability to take responsibility for yourself. That's right...yourself. The lion's share of your success will come from your ability to manage YOU! This chapter is going to outline some of the skills and attributes that will allow you to push through the inevitable challenges of life so you can achieve your destiny. Living a passionate life is what will make you successful and happy. It will be the ability to be persistent and have an undying determination through the challenges of life that will keep your passion alive long enough to bear fruit. Let's look at what you can do to keep your passion alive through persistence and determination.

A LESSON IN PERSISTENCE

Persistence and determination are very important keys to lifelong success. Let's face it; we will all have setbacks if we try enough things in life. I learned the lesson of persistence and determination from the man that I respect most in this world, my father, Jim Rowley.

My dad's career was in managing the operations of a New York City school building. In the winter, when it got cold, my father or one of his employees would have to go in and heat the building so the pipes wouldn't freeze and burst. When I was a young man, my dad had pneumonia and couldn't leave the house. During my dad's illness, we had a pretty bad blizzard. Well, one particular day during the blizzard, the employee assigned to heating the building so the pipes did not freeze decided to give my dad a hard time and refused to go into work. He used the blizzard as his excuse, even though he only lived a few blocks away. This employee *knew* my dad was home with pneumonia. He also knew that my dad was a diligent man who would come in to heat the building, even with pneumonia, if no one else could in order to protect his building. Knowing this, my mom asked me if I would go in. My mom was always in the background nudging us on and allowing our dad to think it was our idea. I asked my dad if he wanted me to go heat up the building and he agreed, although he was a little hesitant. Because he had such an incredible work ethic, he didn't want me to take on his responsibility. He had confidence in me because he knew he had trained me well. I had gone into work with my dad since I was a young child and he was always teaching me something.

Once I got into the building, I tried everything but I couldn't get the boiler going at all. I called my dad and told him I could not get the boilers fired up. It had been over an hour and I just could not get it going. He told me that I hadn't tried everything since it didn't start, so keep trying. A few hours later, I called him again. This time I was angry and short tempered. My dad simply told me that his employee had probably come in and made sure that I couldn't get the boilers going so that we would see just how valuable an employee he was. My dad told me to trace every oil line, steam line, water line and electrical line and to check every safety valve and mechanical mechanism until I figured it out. He said if the other guy could sabotage it, that I could figure it out. These phone calls went on all day and my dad very calmly told me that if he told me what to do, I wouldn't learn anything. He told me to calmly think through the problem and systematically proceed to solve the challenge, to not give up and to persist until I was successful.

A few hours later, I called my dad again, but this time, it was a victory phone call. Boy, was I excited. He told me that he knew I could do it and that now I would know that I "could go about solving any problem I was ever faced with" in life. This lesson has stuck with me through many business set-backs which would have crushed someone else. Someone who didn't have such a smart father, who was willing to take the time to teach his son a very valuable lesson, even though he could have solved the problem in five minutes over the phone with much less hassle and aggravation.

My mom was no different. One time, I joined a basketball team and practice ended up being on the opposite side of town. The coach was a guy that I didn't like or get along with. With practice being so far away, I had to walk or take my bike at least 5 miles in the New York winter cold and snow to get there. I wanted to quit, but my mother made it very clear that quitting wasn't an option. I would have to fulfill my obligations regardless of whether I liked it or not. My whole childhood was like this. *I had two tough Brooklyn parents that were more interested in my character than my comfort.* Thanks Dad and Mom! I am where I am today because you would never let me quit and you built me up from the inside out.

THE POWER OF DETERMINATION

"We all have dreams. But in order to make dreams come into reality, it takes an awful lot of determination, dedication, self-discipline, and effort." —JESSE OWENS

As a boy, I started reading stories that would ignite my spirit and spur me on. These stories were always about real people and the power of the human spirit and how they overcame great obstacles to achieve greatness. One of these stories still stands out in my mind, some 35 years later as an example of what we can achieve when we don't give up.

A little six year old boy had the job of heating his tiny country schoolhouse with his older brother, Floyd. They came in early before their teacher and classmates so the building was warm when the others arrived. One February morning in 1916, the kerosene container had accidentally been filled with gasoline. The stove exploded killing Floyd. This little boy was dragged out of the flaming building barely alive. He had incredible burns brutalizing the lower half of his body.

From his hospital bed, the painfully burned, semi-conscious little boy faintly overheard the doctor telling his mother that her son "would surely die, which was for the best because the poor little boy would surely be a cripple." But this boy wasn't quitting! He made up his mind then and there that he would survive.

Every day his mother would massage his little lifeless legs, but there was no feeling, no control, nothing. Yet, his determination that he would walk was as strong as ever. When he wasn't in bed, he was confined to a wheelchair. One sunny day, his mother wheeled him out into the yard to get some fresh air. But this day was different. Instead of sitting there, he threw himself from the chair. He pulled himself across the grass, dragging his lifeless legs behind him. He worked his way to the white picket fence and with painstaking effort he pulled himself up holding onto the fence. Then, he proceeded to drag himself along the fence, determined that he would walk again. There was nothing he wanted more than to develop life in those legs.

Through his mother's daily massaging of his legs, his unwavering persistence and his resolute determination, he did develop the ability to stand up, then to walk with assistance, then to walk by himself---and then---to run.

And run he did. This little boy, who was told he would never walk again, made the track team in college. Then, one day in Madison Square Garden, this young man who was not expected to survive, who would absolutely never walk, who could never ever dream of running... this determined young man... Glenn Cunningham... ran the world's fastest mile!

This story exemplifies what this book is about. Set your mind to something and put all your energy into it and the world will not deny you! In fact, the world will somehow help!

WRITE THE LAST CHAPTER **FIRST!!!**

Just about every motivational self-help seminar I have been to, book I have read or tape I have ever listened to has had this concept in it. Some say begin with the end in mind, others tell you to write down what you would like your eulogy to be at your funeral, yet others encourage you to imagine you are a fly on the wall at your own funeral overhearing what your friends and loved ones are saying about you now that you are gone. There is a good reason to do this. You need to be living your life in such a way that you are not only achieving your goals, but you are also becoming the person you want to be. Life is not just getting what you want. Life is also a journey of self-discovery. What you become along the way is much more important than what you accumulate.

This concept of writing the last chapter first also works with your energy. We all have beliefs and values that guide us. *If we operate outside our belief and value-system we dig into our own energy reserves.* Our spirits don't feel right and we have a constant tug when we are not doing the right thing or living according to our own beliefs and values. If we don't correct this, it becomes an energy drain that can only be plugged by setting your life straight.

I had just returned from the funeral of a very successful man. He left a legacy that most men would love to leave. The man's name is Charles Cox. Today, at his funeral it became abundantly clear to me what this chapter is all about; why we must write the last chapter first. We have no idea when our last day will be, so we must live the life we want to live every day without compromise. Charles touched the lives of many and the end of his story was truly the beginning of his story.

He was very successful at work, but that wasn't enough for Charles. Today people told story after story of how Charles affected their lives. I don't know how he found time to work or to raise his wonderful family! Charles left behind five incredible sons. His wife, Heath, was loved, cherished and adored by her husband and he taught their boys how to honor and love their mother. Charles was taken from his family way too soon but he didn't waste his time here, he was busy fulfilling his purpose in life. His life continues to bear fruit in the lives he touched and through his wife and sons. He ran the good race and won.

OPTIMISM

One of the things I learned the hard way was that
it doesn't pay to get discouraged.
Keeping busy and making optimism a way of life can restore your faith in yourself.
—LUCILLE BALL

<u>*Life is 10 percent what happens to you and 90 percent how you respond to it.*</u> Refuse to let what happens to you determine your attitude. Most people are like a boat adrift in the ocean getting tossed around by every wave that hits it. They get tossed from problem to problem. They don't respond, they just get tossed around through life letting the rough seas of life determine their destination. STOP! Stop being a victim to life's storms! Take victory over life's storms. Take control of your life and stop letting other people or circumstances determine your destiny. Optimism is one

of life's rudders. Optimism is the daily choice you make BEFORE you get hit in the face by life's next wave. Optimism keeps you on course when the waves of life try to distract you. Be the captain of your own life!

Sir Edmund Hillary was the first man to climb Mount Everest. On May 29, 1953 he reached the summit of the highest mountain then known to man, a staggering 29,000 feet straight up. He was even knighted for his efforts. This didn't happen without obstacles, failure and most importantly an optimistic outlook. In 1952, he attempted to climb Mount Everest but failed. A few weeks later, a group in England asked him to address its members. Hillary walked on stage to a thunderous applause. The audience was recognizing an attempt at greatness, but Edmund Hillary knew he wasn't done with Mount Everest. He wasn't interested in just an attempt. He wanted to conquer the unconquerable mountain. Slowly he moved away from the microphone and walked deliberately to the edge of the platform. He shook his fist and pointed at a picture of the mountain and said, *"Mount Everest, you beat me the first time, but I'll beat you the next time because you've grown all you are going to grow... but I'm still growing!"* Boy! Did he get his "Brooklyn up"!" (That is what my tough 102 years old grandmother says when she's been pushed enough to push back...HARD. Real HARD!)

Are you still growing or are you letting the Mount Everest's in your life win? The choice is yours. I think since you have gotten this far in this book, that you are not only a fighter, you're a conqueror! Put this book down right now and walk over to the imaginary picture of *"your Mount Everest"* and get your *"Brooklyn up""* big time! Shake your fist at it in defiance and tell it *"you beat me the first time, but I'll beat you the next time because you've grown all you are going to grow... but I'm still growing!"* Now I'm not kidding. Put this book down and challenge that mountain! Go ahead. Get your "Brooklyn up". This is your life. No one is looking and if they are, so what! People from Brooklyn don't care who is looking at them. Be defiant because you WILL conquer that mountain. Let the world know that you will continue to grow and defeat all the Mount Everest's in your life. You are a winner. Now the mountain knows it and so do you!

MOTIVATION FROM THE MASTERS

Now that you have made the choice to continue growing, the key is to know what you focus on, what you put in your mind. Your mind is like a computer. What you put in is what will come out. If you regularly put in positive and uplifting thoughts what comes out will be the same. I am not telling you to brain wash yourself with foolishly positive thoughts as though you are living in a fantasy world. I am saying to invite positive, uplifting thoughts into your head. One way to do this is by spending time with the masters of motivation on a daily basis.

When my son John was about 15 years old, we'd had about enough. He was always a handful, to say the least. One year, he was grounded for the whole year---one day at a time. I think it was harder on my wife and me than it was on him! He was constantly misbehaving in school, not doing his homework, talking back, trying to go where ever he wanted WHEN ever he wanted and in general just not going by our rules. His attitude was negative about everything. We had tried everything to get through to him. At one point my wife, Cathy, decided to make him listen to my Zig Ziglar "How to Stay Motivated" tape series. Every night before bed, he had to listen to Zig for 30 minutes. Boy did he complain! It was like we were making him drink battery acid! We enforced it and then the unexpected happened. Within two or three days, Johnny's whole attitude changed. We found out that he not only did the 30 minutes every night, he did more than an hour. Within a couple of days, every time he got hit with one of life's waves, instead of responding the "old" way, he quoted old Zig! We couldn't believe it. He even had Zig's accent down (although Zig denies having an accent.) He LOVED Zig and would keep quoting him day after day. What he was doing was filling his mind with positive and uplifting thoughts and what came out was more of the same.

I contacted Mr. Ziglar's office and his assistant Laurie Magers told me that Mr. Ziglar was thrilled that the results were so wonderful, but added that he hated to be the boy's punishment, she did tell me the last part with a chuckle. By the way, today John is a husband and a father. His focus, motivation and faith in himself allowed him to buy his first home at 20 years old. AWESOME! Even now, when he is struggling he still pops in a tape of Zig. Actually, he listens to different motivational tapes all of the time, but Zig is still his all time favorite.

In fact, I listen to tapes and CD's all the time. How do you think Cathy came up with the idea to make John listen to those tapes? She knew what listening to motivational tapes has done for me. I know it is hard to believe, but I am a handful also. I listen to tapes and CD's all of the time. I never listen to the radio. The most important feature that I look for in a new car is that it has a tape player and a CD player so I can continue to fill my own mind with motivation from the masters!

John with motivational speaker, author and President of High Point University Nido Qubein

Through books, tapes and CD's you have the opportunity to be continually mentored by the best of the best. Listen to the great motivational speakers. Fill your mind with positive and uplifting thoughts and that is what will come out when you need it. In fact, some authors/mentors will even spend some time with you if you just ask. While preparing this book, I asked legendary Nido Qubein for 15 minutes of his time to pick his brain and Nido generously gave me an hour and a half!

POSITIVE SELF TALK

Positive self talk is one of the most powerful things you can do to keep yourself motivated. I know you have probably heard all of this before, but perhaps you don't fully realize just how important "self-talk" is to changing your life and defining who you are. You are who you tell yourself you are. What you say to yourself is so much more important than what anyone else says to you.

When I was in my 20's, I worked in a New York City School as a janitor. I would be around guys that were doing as little as they could, without losing their jobs. They put more effort into NOT working than it would have taken to just do the job properly. I remember one guy. He was smart and had all the right tools but he continually talked himself out of success. He would say things like, "The boss will never promote me. He will bring in a friend from the outside." "I will never get that position. I have been here for over 10 years and I have never gotten it, so why would I get it now?"

Man, I would listen to this and try to reason with him but all he had was negativity and reasons why he couldn't do something. I got sick of listening to his poison, so I stayed away from him. In less than a year, I got the position he wanted. I got it because I came in on my free time to learn the job. When the position abruptly became available, I was the only one who knew how to do it. Even though they didn't want to promote me, I got the position anyway. I'd always told myself I would get the job and because I had spoken to myself in a motivating way, I didn't mind going in on my time for free, and "earning" the position even before it became available. Let me say that again. I earned the position. It wasn't given to me! I earned it and talked myself into earning it.

We talk to ourselves all the time, without really realizing it. So we may as well say things that are going to help us, instead of hurt us. Many of us are in the habit of negative "self-talk", like my co-worker was. For example, we say things like, "Dummy! Only I could be so stupid! I am so fat, no wonder no one wants me! I am horrible, ugly, undeserving, a failure, etc. etc." And let's not forget my all time favorite "It's all my fault, I can't do anything right!" We get into a habit of talking down to ourselves, instead of lifting ourselves up. You wouldn't let anyone else talk to you this way, so why do you talk to yourself this way? What do you have against you?

The cool thing is that our subconscious mind does not know the difference between self-talk and reality. If we say something to ourselves enough times, we believe it. What happens when we believe it? It becomes reality. So, let's talk ourselves into lives of passion so we can live the lives of our dreams.

Positive self-talk is, also called positive affirmations. You can literally change your life by repeating positive affirmations over and over again to yourself. Don't worry if you don't believe them yet. You will in time. Now, I am not talking about Stuart Smalley's affirmations from Saturday Night live, *"I'm good enough,*

I'm smart enough, and doggone it, people like me." Not that there is anything wrong with those words, it was just meant as a goof. There is nothing goofy about positive affirmations. They can and will change your life. Remember, that the opinion you have of yourself is much more important than the opinion anyone else has of you and the most important conversations you will ever have are the conversations you have with yourself. The key is to design those conversations so they support you.

You can write your own affirmations, look some up online or get affirmations out of the bible or another inspirational book. Just make sure that you write them for yourself. Personalize them by adding your name and speaking them to yourself in the first person. If you are writing out your own affirmations, write them in the present tense as if they are already true. Also, don't say, "I am no longer fat." Say instead, "I am fit and I feel incredible." Always include as much feeling as you can. Use your body by standing up. Get excited and look at yourself in the mirror as you say them. Get all of your senses involved and you will see better results. Here are some sample affirmations:

- I enjoy exercising daily and eating properly. I feel incredibly fit, strong and energetic.

- I am moving forward in my career because I give more than I receive.

- I'm looking and feeling better every day because I have a lifestyle that supports me!

- I jump out of bed early in the morning and I feel incredible and energetic. I look forward to my day because I am prepared, enthusiastic and passionate about what I do! I am more than a conqueror!

Some final tips:

- Say your affirmation just before bed, your subconscious mind will work on it while you sleep.
- Repeat your affirmations in the morning before you start your day.
- Record your affirmations into a tape recorder and listen to them in the car, bus, train or plane.
- Your affirmations should always be in the positive and as if it has already happened.

When you replace your negative thoughts with positive thoughts, you catapult yourself to success. Try it for yourself and enjoy the immediate results.

Choose to be happy

Most folks are about as happy as they
make up their minds to be. —Abraham Lincoln

Old Abe was right. Make up your mind to be happy! Who decides whether or not you will be happy? That's right, the answer is you! Being optimistic and happy is a daily choice. It is not an emotion we wait to feel or something we wait around for so that when the situation is right we can get ecstatic about our lives. In fact, if we let our situations dictate our attitude, I guarantee most of the time we won't be optimistic, happy or joyful! We have the power to choose our response to every situation in life---GOOD or BAD. So why not choose to be happy?

When I was first starting out in real estate, I had to walk a few miles to the closest subway station. I then got on the jam-packed subway with my nice suit (which was, in fact, my only suit at the time) and squeezed in with all of the masses. It was horrible, humbling and ironic to say the least. Once at work, I was an executive, but on the way to work, I was fighting for my spot on the cattle car. The subway smelled and I had to stand the whole way. I was squashed and pushed with every turn of the subway. It was very hard to be upbeat and happy when I arrived at work after my "subway" experience.

I chose not to let the trip to work ruin my day. In fact, I was determined to make good use of the time on the subway. I decided to record my affirmations reminding myself everything I was happy and thankful for and I listened to the tape on the subway. I also kept a motivational tape with me at all times. Once I was done with my affirmation tape, I would pop in one of my "mentors" and have a great time having my meeting with my own personal mentor. My subway trip turned from something that I hated into something that I looked forward to. Take the things in your life that you dread, that steal your joy and turn them into something positive or productive the way I did with the subway. Remember what Abraham Lincoln said, *"Most folks are about as happy as they make up their minds to be."* Make up your mind to be happy, starting today and see your life change for the better!

BELIEVE IT IS POSSIBLE

Think, Believe, Dream, Dare —WALT DISNEY

This quote by Walt Disney has been hanging on my office wall for decades. Also, in my office, are two other things that are important to me. One is a check that paid my membership many years ago to join R&J Health Studio, LONG before I realized my dream of owning it. The other thing is a jar of coal my Dad gave me for Christmas. I know it sounds like an odd combination but let me explain. All of the above are there because I was bold enough to take the challenge from Walt Disney to *Think, Believe, Dream and Dare.*

I grew up being told not to dream. *"You are such a dreamer, why don't you grow up!"* I would be told time and time again as a child. Then, when I got older and had a family, I constantly had people close to me reminding me that I shouldn't dream. I had a family to support. I was being selfish and childish. I was not smart enough, educated enough or good enough to do the things I wanted to achieve. I should just settle for my lot in life. People will discourage you in something, because they know they can't do it. Let me tell you right now, if you are hearing things like that, don't listen! Those words are right out of the pit of hell. Let no man dictate what you can and cannot do. You were created for greatness. I am very fortunate that the most important person in my life, my beautiful wife, Cathy, has always encouraged me and told me to focus on my dreams and to be all I could be. I am truly blessed with a wonderful encourager for a wife.

The reason I have Walt Disney's quote hanging on my office wall next to the check written to the R&J Health Studio and a jar of coal sitting on my desk, is for a daily reminder to myself that if I DO think, believe, dream and dare, I can achieve what seems to be the impossible. When I was a young man, I talked about owning a gym just like R&J Health Studio and I was constantly shot down by everyone but my wife. She not only encourages me to dream, she tells me to get my butt moving on my dreams (in other words to take action), to put shoe leather to it and to not give up.

Yes, I did buy R&J Health Studio and the years I owned it were some of the best years of my life. The coal on my desk was given to me by my dad. I had just gotten into Manhattan real estate at William B. May on Madison Avenue and that very Christmas, Dad gave me and my brothers each a jar of coal to remind us of our family roots. My dad's ancestors were coal miners in Pennsylvania. But for me it held an additional meaning. One of my duties while working in a New York City Public School was to shovel coal into boilers to heat the building; A LOT of coal. Not only did I shovel the coal into the boiler, but I had to bring the coal from the coal pit to the boiler. Then, after the coal was burned, I had to clean out all the ash, put it into the ash cans and bring the ash cans up out to the street for pick up. It was physically exhausting, filthy work. I kept that jar of coal on my desk as a reminder, that regardless of how many challenges I may have in the business world, it could be worse. I could be back in the boiler room breathing in coal dust and shoveling coal into a boiler. There is nothing wrong with shoveling coal, it is good honest work, but the thought leaves me with a bad taste in my mouth (pun not intended). You see, I had people telling me that I should be doing just that--ONLY that--all the while, trying to discourage me from trying to "conquer the world". For me, I would rather not have to do it again,....ever.

Most people are not being malicious when they try to discourage you from striving for outstanding success. They are just voicing their own fears. To them, failure is the worst thing that can happen. To ME, failure is simply a part of success. Let them keep their fear and negativity, I don't want any part of it and neither should you.

I once heard that Walt Disney wouldn't even take on a project unless every person on his board of directors told him *not to do it!* You heard right…*not to do it!* He believed that if everyone agreed with him, that he wasn't thinking big enough. He also said, *"We did it (referring to Disneyland), in the knowledge that most of the people I talked to, thought it would be a financial disaster - closed and forgotten within the first year."* Good thing for us old Walt didn't listen to those people.

On December 15, 2005 I copied the New York Times Best Sellers List and I put this in the #1 spot. <u>**"CLIMB YOUR LADDER OF SUCCESS WITHOUT RUNNING OUT OF GAS!,** by John M. Rowley. The simple truth on how to revitalize your body and ignite your energy for lifelong success!"</u> I made a copy of the list, framed it and hung it on my wall to look at every day. Once I contracted with my publisher, I emailed it to him to make sure we had the same vision. Once, I even had someone come into my office and congratulate me on the success of my book and this was before I even had a publisher. I just thanked him in faith knowing that it would happen. You are reading these words because I dared to think you would, believed you would and dreamed that you would one day be holding this book! What should you be doing that you are holding back on, out of fear? What great dream have you had that others told you was impossible or that you were even nuts to even consider? If Walt Disney is any example, the very things you *"aren't"* doing may be your road to greatness. Go for it! Pursue your dreams with passion.

BELIEVE IN YOURSELF

God didn't have time to make a nobody, only a somebody.
I believe that each of us has God-given talents within us waiting
to be brought to fruition. —MARY KAY ASH

I don't know about you, but sometimes I can look at people around me and know that they can achieve anything they put their minds to, but when I look at myself, I have a nagging doubt. I think most people go through this at times. The difference between the successful and the unsuccessful is that the successful person only allows this to be a fleeting thought. You must believe in yourself and have faith in your abilities! Without a humble and reasonable belief in your abilities, you are sunk before you set sail.

Today you hear of so many people with self-esteem problems or inferiority complexes. I want to say to them, "STOP!!!!!". Stop feeling sorry for yourself. Stop lamenting over what someone has said about you or to you. Stop worrying about yesterday. Stop giving permission for someone who mistreated you in the past to ruin your future.

Yes, I know some people have had traumatic and hideous things done to them. But just because someone hurt you in the past doesn't mean you should give them permission to ruin your future. Some things do require professional help to get past and if you need it, I suggest you get it. Remember that we become what we focus on all the time. If you are focusing on past hurts or disappointments you will have trouble in your present and future.

Many of the self defeating thoughts we have stem from childhood. Maybe I can illustrate this by sharing part of my childhood with you. Growing up I was painfully thin. I was the last to be picked when there were pick-up games in the park and was at the bottom of my class academically. Can't you feel my pain? Only joking, it didn't bother me too much because I knew who I was and where I was going.

School, however, was probably the toughest environment for me. I was a very active, high energy kid who was extremely bored with the painfully slow moving classroom. I went to a private school and I endured physical and mental punishment at the hands of the teachers. Ruthless and heartless describes my memories of those first eight years. I was determined not to let them get to me. The teachers would hit my knuckles with a yard stick and when that wouldn't make me cry, they would hit my finger tips, turning my finger nails black and blue in an effort to break me. They never broke me. I stayed happy, telling myself that I would be something one day, regardless of how stupid and bad they told me I was. As you can imagine, it wasn't the most encouraging or uplifting environment.

I must admit, it wasn't all one-sided or undeserved. I did find ways to get back at them. One Friday afternoon, we were going through the walk-thru coat closet before leaving for the weekend. At the end of the closet, just before exiting, there was a large walk-in cage where the teacher kept her personal belongings. Well, I was the last one exiting the closet that fine day. All of the sudden, I felt my hand reach in and close the cage, locking the teacher in. She never even saw me. I was thrilled for about fifteen minutes, and then I began to feel very bad. I walked back to school and found Mr. Donovan, the school's janitor. I told him what I'd done expecting the worst. What I got was a hearty belly laugh and then he told me, "Laddie, never you mind. I will let her out…eventually", as he laughed again. "It might do the old goat some good", he added. When I came back to school Monday, I was expecting the wrath from hell, but Mr. Donovan never told our secret. Instead, this teacher was very humble and not quite as mean for the rest of the year.

One thing I noticed through the years was that the kids who excelled in that particular grade school did nothing in the real world afterward. Likewise, other kids that were tormented by the teachers, like I was, went on not doing much either. I'm not sure where they are today, but in high school some got into drugs and others into trouble. The teachers won. They broke those kids, who then gave up on life. I am not saying that I have all the answers but I know one thing, I wasn't about to give permission to those teachers to ruin my life. All they could ruin was the time I had in their school. I didn't allow them to define who I was. Don't let your past define who you are! The future is yours. Take control of it and let go of the past.

The only reason I bring this up is to let you know that we all have things to overcome. One of the best ways I know to get beyond this is with forgiveness. Forgive the people who harmed you. Forgive yourself for the harm you brought upon yourself. Overflow your mind with faith. Develop a tremendous faith and this will bring you confidence in yourself, but it will be a humble confidence, because you know that you didn't create yourself. Let's take a look at the steps toward taking control of your future by letting go of your past.

THE POWER OF FORGIVENESS

Forgive your enemies, but never forget their names.
—JOHN F. KENNEDY

Don't you love that? *Forgive your enemies, but never forget their names.*" Just because you forgive someone doesn't mean you need to forget that they may be bad for you. I know we are to love everyone, but I can't find anywhere that we must "like" everyone. Forgiveness is a conscious decision and sometimes a daily conscious decision. We may think that forgiveness is a gift to the person that has wronged us. Wrong! Wrong! Wrong! Oh, did you hear me? WRONG! Forgiveness is for the forgiver. You not forgiving someone is like you poisoning yourself and expecting the other person to die! It's not happening. The only person you are hurting is yourself.

Forgiveness is for you and it's simple. Simply ask yourself, "Am I willing to waste my time and energy on someone who doesn't have my best interest at heart?" "Am I willing to give that person the permission to ruin my day?" If the answer is "No" then that's it! Consciously forgive that person and get on with it. If you find yourself thinking about the situation, then forgive the person again and again and eventually the forgiveness will stick.

> *Forgive all who have offended you, not for them,*
> *but for yourself.* —HARRIET NELSON

I had a personal problem with forgiveness a few years ago. I had a difficult time forgiving someone and my wife and my pastor both told me that I needed to forgive this man for my own sake. He didn't deserve forgiveness they told me, but I had to do it for my own sake. This didn't mean that I forget what he did or even give him an opportunity to do it again. It just meant that I needed to forgive him. Even with this encouragement, I couldn't forgive him. I tried…and failed.

I knew I needed to forgive this man and I eventually got to the point where I was able to forgive him. I had to forgive him every day, several times a day, every day, until it started to stick. Once I was able to forgive him, I felt much better. I was able to shove the weight of hate and resentment off of my shoulders. Like I said earlier, forgiveness is for the forgiver! I learned this one the hard way.

The power of prayer

Forgiveness is very important and so is developing a dynamic life changing faith. The way to do this is through prayer. I am not talking about babbling prayer. I am talking about a conversation with your Creator. Talk to Him the way you would talk to your best friend. And be bold, most prayers aren't big enough. Pray big prayers, because we have a big God. As your faith grows, you will find that you believe in yourself more. I know faith is a very personal thing and I also know that there is no down side to believing in God and letting Him work in your life. When you have faith that God is at work in your life, you can be much more confident in believing in yourself.

We all have times in our life when we just want to throw our hands up in the air and give up. We wake up in the morning, dreading the day because we don't know what to do. Recently, my wife and I were having problems in our business. Plus, our kids were all growing into young adults and some were not making some of the wisest choices. Quite honestly, some of the choices we were making in response to these situations were poor, also. We were at the end of our rope and just wanted to give up. Instead of giving up, we gave it to God. Immediately, we felt better and within days our children were progressing nicely and the answers for our business challenges seemed to appear out of thin air. The bottom line is, we have little control over what happens to us but we have complete control over how we respond and prayer is the best response to the troubled waters in life.

Several years ago, a friend of mine returned from Kazakhstan. He looked dejected and beat. When I asked him what was going on, he told me about a mutual Kazak friend, Danyar, who had broken his leg in a motorcycle accident. The way the Kazakh hospital had repaired the leg was with a regular drill that was not sterilized. They then told the him to walk on his leg immediately. Over in Kazakhstan, they believe you must walk on a broken leg immediately in order for it to heal. Unfortunately, Danyar was walking in a spot that had been freshly mopped and slipped and broke the same leg in a different spot, so they had to drill on his leg again. Both surgeries on his leg were performed without anesthesia. They told him if he screamed they would stop and let him bleed to death. The bottom line is, by the time my friend got over to Kazakhstan, Danyar had gangrene.

My friend had returned home just days before I'd spoken to him. He was very depressed because it seemed certain that Danyar was going to die. I told him that God has a plan, has always been in the healing business and I suggested we continue to pray, ask God to heal him and see what happens. Within minutes of praying, we got an idea to contact another friend to let him know what was going on. With an idea in mind, Jim started the ball in motion. He spoke to some others and was able to arrange free medical care at Duke University. Through grants and donations, this young man was in the United States getting the medical care he needed within a few weeks. It took many surgeries and a long recovery but this young man is now serving his countrymen in Kazakhstan just because a couple of guys prayed a big prayer.

GOING TO FAILURE

Failure is a detour, not a dead end street. —ZIG ZIGLAR

"Going to failure" is what athletes strive for in the gym when lifting weights. It is when you can't possibly get another rep or move the weight anymore. In other words, you have completely failed to go any further. You really see results in the gym in terms of strength and in how your body looks when you can push yourself to the point of failure. It is a very positive thing in the gym. In the gym, "going to failure" brings great results in muscle growth and strength. Likewise, real success comes when you can bring that attitude into the real world. Most times, success is the result of "going to failure" many times. In the gym, you can have someone help you when the weight gets too heavy. This person is called a spotter. In life, you rarely have the luxury of a spotter when you fail. **<u>Your attitude toward failure is your spotter!</u>**

If I can point to one thing in my life that allowed me to be a success, it is the fact that I don't let failure overtake me or keep me down. In fact, I memorized a quote from Og Mandino that I repeat often. *"Failure will never overtake me if my determination to succeed is strong enough"*. I also memorized another quote by the famous sales trainer, Tom Hopkins, that I also repeated more times than I would like to admit. *"I am not judged by the number of times I fail, but by the number of times I succeed; and the number of times I succeed is in direct proportion to the number of times I can fail and keep on trying."* Read those again out loud to yourself because that is the key to success!

I remember one time I had to close down a business. It was very hard for me to close this business. Not only did I have all of our money and some of my parents' money tied up in it, but my wife and I had our hearts tied-up in it. This was a hard one, but I dragged myself up, dusted myself off and got on to the next thing. A man close to my family didn't think I felt bad enough because I got going again too easily in his eyes. He decided to point out to me how much of a failure I was and how much I failed my family. I disagreed and told him that I learned much more closing my business than I did while I was operating it. I told him, tongue in cheek and in an effort to stay positive, that I was getting my masters degree in the business world and learning a ton. He told me that I wasn't getting a masters degree, that I wasn't smart enough for that and that I was simply a failure! He said that I should give up and just go back to being a janitor. Unfortunately, this is the way some people think. If you have people like this in your life, just know you can't count on them to lift you up and encourage you when you need it the most. You do, however, need to have encouragers around you and the time to find them is before you need them. Your greatest encourager is your own positive outlook and the knowledge that you will fail while pursuing success. That is just part of the game.

A few years ago, I bought some real estate with a partner and he didn't live up to his end of the bargain. It took two years to work itself out and I ended up on the short end of the stick. Was I angry and disappointed? You bet! I would be lying if I said I wasn't. But was I defeated? ABSOLUTELY NOT! In fact, it spurred me on and within months I had put together a lucrative real estate deal that paid me handsomely and immediately. All parties came out winners.

Success and failure aren't opposites, they're neighbors separated by a thin line…by a single decision. The decision NOT TO QUIT! Success requires resilience in the face of failure. Failure is part of success and the feedback from failure is a great education. Let failure guide you, not cripple you. The way to use failure to your benefit is by following these simple steps.

1. Know it is just part of the process and that you did the best you could with what you had at the time.

2. Write down what you learned and change or adjust your next approach if necessary.

3. Take time to review your past successes. It is important to remind yourself of your successes.

4. Take immediate action on something positive leading to your goal.

5. Stay focused on the ultimate outcome, not the short term set backs.

6. Don't give up!!

Remember what Theodore Roosevelt said. *"He who makes no mistakes makes no progress."* Welcome the failures because they lead to the successes. Now, go to failure in all areas of your life so you will have great success in and out of the gym.

EXPECT SUCCESS AND GET IT

This young boy was constantly told, "Why you can't be like this person or that person? Why can't you do in good school? You should be more like Jimmy around the block. He gets great grades!" For many years his old report cards were kept in a handy kitchen drawer so they could be taken out at any given time as a reminder of how useless he was. The grade school teachers reinforced this by putting him in all the "special" classes and telling him that he would never measure up to the other kids. In fact, he was told by the teachers that he shouldn't even go to high school; that he wasn't high school material. All of this was probably done to spur the boy on, but constantly being reminded of failure and short comings seldom lifts people to success.

In eighth grade, this young boy was sitting on the side lines watching a CYO track meet. He was just watching his friends and playing around with his lacrosse stick. The track coach came over and told him that he must run the 440 yard dash. The boy protested and said that he didn't know how to run, was wearing work boots and jeans and really didn't want to run. The coach was persistent and persuasive so the boy agreed to run.

There he was, with his heart in his throat. He looked like an idiot standing there on the starting line with work boots and jeans among all the runners wearing their uniforms and track shoes. He then looked at the coach and said "What do I do?" The coach simply told him, "Stay close to the other boys and when you get to the sewer cap on the other side of the track to run as fast as you can." The boy nodded, the gun went off and the boys were running. This boy was in the back of the pack for the first 50 or 60 yards but decided to jog up to the front runner. When he got up close to the guy in the lead and said, "Coach said that once we jog to the sewer cap, the race begins." It was cool. It was like the trotters at the race track, when the horses jog behind the car for a while." The other boy, however, was not amused and huffing and puffing, couldn't speak at all. To make a long story short, when they got to the sewer cap this boy took off, leaving all the other runners very far behind. He crossed the finish line to learn that the race didn't begin at the sewer cap. It began when the gun went off. And the other boys weren't jogging; they were going as fast as they could. This boy qualified for the state championship and the unexpected happened, his grades in school went up. His whole life changed because now he expected success in all areas of his life. He discovered he wasn't less than anyone else, he just may learn a little differently.

That little boy was me. Once I found out that I was good in one thing, it carried over to all areas of my life. I expected more of myself than anyone would ever ask of me. From that point on, I expected to be successful. And you know what? I was. I still wasn't an "A" student, but I knew that I could be if I wanted to be.

Expect the best and you will get it, but the reverse is also true. If you are expecting the worst you will not be disappointed.

STOP WORRYING

Some people are just not happy unless they are worrying about something. Many times these same people are even more "joyous" when they can infect you with their anxiety. If you have someone like this in your life, keep them at arms length. If you are a worry wart, stop right now! Worry is the enemy of peace. I would much rather have the fresh fruit of peace than the rotting fruit of worry, wouldn't you?

> *Most fears cannot withstand the test of careful scrutiny and analysis.*
> *When we expose our fears to the light of thoughtful examination*
> *they usually just evaporate.* —JACK CANFIELD

My grandfather was a wonderful and loving man. When I was a young boy, he was always the one laughing the loudest and telling the jokes. Walking down the streets near his home in Brooklyn, he knew everyone and had a smile for them all. Then one day, this all changed. I am not quite sure what happened, but he started to be fearful and worry all the time. He wouldn't burden us with his worries; he just quietly sat in the corner, twiddled his thumbs and slowly, quietly, worried himself to death. I couldn't have asked for a better grandfather, but sadly he began to focus on something that made him worry and it killed him and then he died. The reason I said it killed him and then he died is because his spirit was dead years before his body.

Faith and fear (worry) are not good roommates. One must move out in order for the other to take residence. So if you want to get fear to move out, invite faith into your life. Make up your mind not to worry beforehand. This is a key to stopping the worry habit. Before you are in the position that causes you to worry, have a plan of attack. Make it an act of your conscious will and if you catch yourself worrying, take your thoughts captive and start speaking empowering self talk to yourself. Remind yourself who you are. All of these things will work and work like a champ!

Action Steps

Remember, the world doesn't reward us for what we know;
it rewards us for what we do!

1. Decide what you want your life to stand for.
2. Life is 10 percent what happens to you and 90 percent how you respond. Be prepared. Decide your responses in advance.
3. Start listening to the Masters of Motivation. Get mentored by the best in the areas you want to succeed in.
4. Put positive self talk to work in your life. Write the affirmations that you want to empower you on a 3X5 card and repeat them at least three times per day.
5. Choose to be happy. Like Abe Lincoln said, make up your mind to be happy.

6. Think, Believe, Dream, Dare. Believe it is possible.

7. Forgive and let go of your past.

8. Replace worry with faith.

CHAPTER

$$\boxed{3}$$

Passion: The Engine of Success

ENTHUSIASM

Nothing great was ever achieved without enthusiasm.

—RALPH WALDO EMERSON

Enthusiasm is the key to all success. In fact, the word enthusiasm has its root in the Greek word *enthousiasmos, to be inspired by God.* Man, living a life that is inspired by God would keep you enthusiastic, wouldn't it? The bottom line is, when you know in your heart why you are here, you will be excited about getting "to it". You will be passionate about fulfilling your destiny! That passion is the engine that drives the success in your life.

I have known many people over the years that have made a ton of money, but were still unhappy. I am sure you know some people like that also. I also know people that make little money, but are fulfilled and enthusiastic about life. Obviously dollar signs are not the sign of success. Ross Patterson works more hours than most successful business people who make very substantial incomes. He also travels the world constantly. I can get an email from him one day and he is in China, the next in the UK and yet a couple of days later he is in Singapore and then in New York. Ross and his wife Christine are Christian workers and are passionate about what they do. Their enthusiasm for life and for their purpose in life is infectious. You cannot be around them without being lifted up. Ross is one of my mentors and even though he is the busiest person I know, he sows into my life more than anyone else. He can do this because of the enthusiasm he has for helping others with his unique gifts. Remember what Zig Ziglar said, *"This I do know beyond any reasonable doubt, regardless of what you are doing, if you pump long enough, hard enough and enthusiastically enough, sooner or later the effort will bring forth the reward."* Get enthusiastic about your life and watch great things happen to you and to those around you! Remember, enthusiasm is infectious. Infect those around you with the enthusiasm bug!

THE POWER OF THOUGHTS

Men are not prisoners of fate, but only prisoners of their own minds.
—FRANKLIN D. ROOSEVELT

Humans have the unique ability to think and dream; to create their own future before it arrives through creative thoughts and dreams. Your subconscious mind doesn't know the difference between something that really happens to you and something you vividly imagine. Haven't you repeated something in your mind so often that you thought it actually happened? I know I have. Athletes and people in all areas of life that are successful have been utilizing visualization to their advantage for years. Vividly imagine your successes, your triumphs, and your victories and before you know it they will be happening.

"Whatever our minds can conceive, we can achieve" is a much used phrase and an accurate one. This is called the law of attraction. You attract to you the very things you think about most. One thing that I have realized in my own life is that anything I have ever accomplished started with a thought that turned into a dream. I was mocked as a kid and told that I was a dreamer. I wish I would have known the power of dreams and of my thoughts back then, because I would have thanked the person mocking me instead of feeling inadequate.

My journey from being a janitor in Brooklyn to conducting business in the real estate board rooms of Madison Avenue, started off as a thought that turned into a dream that I had while pushing a broom in Franklin K. Lane High School in Brooklyn. I then intensified the dream by going to the 59th Street Bridge and while looking at the skyline of Manhattan, I convinced myself that I would conquer Manhattan Real Estate. And yes, people thought I was nuts and didn't hesitate to tell me. Owning R&J Health Studio also started off as a dream that I had while watching the movie Pumping Iron. While Arnold Schwarzenegger and Lou Ferrigno battled it out in Pretoria, South Africa for the Mr. Olympia title, I dreamed of owning "the east coast Mecca of body building", the Brooklyn gym made famous in that movie. My getting involved with the International Federation of Body Building, the National Physique Committee and the fitness industry started off as the dream of a kid who thumbed through the old bodybuilding and fitness magazines. Even this book began as a thought that germinated into a dream and has now bloomed into the book you are reading. *Don't be a prisoner of your own mind, be a pioneer of your own destiny!*

BELIEVE TO ACHIEVE!

People of achievement are people of believe-ment!
—JOHN M. ROWLEY

The real power of your thoughts starts with belief. I know we spoke about belief in Chapter 2, but I think this ties in well here as well. Believe that you are more than a conquer! Doesn't that lift your spirits just reading it? "I am more than a conquer!" Imagine what you could achieve if you repeated it so often that you truly believed it. You are not just a conqueror, but you are more than a conqueror. Believe it with every fiber of your being and you will be unstoppable! You can be the Brave Heart of Wall Street or whatever street you work on.

If you can believe it, you can achieve it. It all starts with the belief that it will come to pass. We usually get what we expect and this works equally as well in the positive as it does in the negative. If you believe something will happen then you will act in such a way to cause it to happen... good or bad it will happen. In fact that is how my friend Brian built his company.

When I first got into Manhattan Real Estate my best friend Brian McLaughlin had a small alarm company on Long Island. We both thought it would be fun to work together in Manhattan plus the opportunities for his business were incredible. So I started giving Brian some small jobs in various buildings that I managed. Every time I asked him if he knew how to do a certain job that I was giving him, he would tell me, "John, don't ask me questions that you don't want the answers to." Then he would laugh and tell me, "John this isn't rocket science, if I don't know how to do it I will either figure it out or find someone who does know how to do it. I will do an incredible job for your building, at the best price possible and isn't that what you want anyway?" Well how could I say no to that!

To make a long story short, I believed in Brian enough to give him a shot, in fact I would play him up as if he were the best company in town. Brian believed in himself so much that he made that shot count. Before long his company was growing like wild fire. Today he is the premier security company in Manhattan. Now the whole city believes in The SecureCom Group. But it all started because Brian expected to succeed with all his heart and wouldn't consider any other option. He believed it long before anyone else could see it.

Job said, *"What I feared has come upon me; what I dreaded has happened to me."* What you focus on will happen. If you are passionate and believe with all your heart that you will have a better, more prosperous life then that will come to pass. I know I can hear you now. "But John, what if I believe it and it doesn't happen?" Yeah, but what if it does? If you believe for something and keep a positive attitude coupled with a sense of expectation, good things will follow. It may not be exactly what you were shooting for, it may be much better.

People of achievement are people of believe-ment. Never forget that. I have never met anyone who was successful that always focused on the negative and expected the worst from life. No just the opposite, they look toward the future with a sense of hope, faith and enthusiasm that what they are working towards will happen.

In 1993, I had a business go under. It was devastating to not only me, but to my wife as well. We'd put our hearts in this venture and this sucked the wind right out of us. I believed that I was more than my business and got moving again. I interviewed for a real estate job in Manhattan and even with all of my contacts, I couldn't get a job. It was a bad time of year. They had no opening, etc. I heard every excuse known to man and I could have let it keep me down. Instead, I got out of my comfort level and took a commission job in brokerage at The Corcoran Group owned by my friend Barbara Corcoran.

Even though my expertise was in management, I gladly walked through this open door. I was confident that opportunity was knocking. However, in order to feed my family, I also reached down to my humble beginnings and worked as a janitor in Harlem. Bundled up and looking like the Michelin Tire Man, I de-iced and shoveled snow from the perimeter of the school grounds before the sun rose in the sky. I then assisted in firing up the boilers and cleaning the building. I worked from the middle of the night to early in the morning, so Barbara allowed me to start a little later then the rest of the brokers to accommodate my schedule. I showered and changed into my suit in the janitor's closet at the school in Harlem and then went to my real estate sales office. No one knew the difference. For all they knew, I was coming from home.

I then made over 200 cold calls a night with no result at all, at first. I was told that it was not appropriate to cold call these exclusive Manhattan apartments. (Side note: My thought was that since everyone else didn't want to prospect, only one broker calling wouldn't bother anyone, plus it would make me stand out. And stand out, it did) Instead of getting discouraged I got more encouraged because I knew if I could keep a positive mindset, I would succeed. I knew I was getting closer to success!

Then it happened. After a few months of cleaning toilets, scrubbing floors and shoveling snow in Harlem followed by endless cold calls, I got my first break to the tune of an $875,000.00 listing which sold quickly. In fact, it sold so quickly that I had a job in management before it closed. This happened because I got back in the game and kept a positive attitude. Everyone thought I was doing great. And you know what? I was! I was enjoying the challenge and knew that I would rise victoriously from the ashes. Also being around all the great people at The Corcoran Group like Barbara Corcoran, Theresa Hall, Elaine Dean, Jeff Levitas and Dan Douglas made it easy to stay positive and had a lasting impact on my life.

An old friend of mine, Al Mayas who is currently Executive Managing Director of Charles H. Greenthal, heard what I was doing, respected my resolve and hired me as a property manager at a company he was running at the time. Within months, I was a director of management for another company and within a few more months, I was Sr. Vice President of yet another company. Al supported me every step of the way and is still a good friend today. It happened very quickly once it started, but it never would have started if I had stayed home and felt sorry for myself. No. I took a step, had faith in myself and hung in there for many long months. Then and only then did it happen quickly. It happened because I knew it would happen and saw it through my eyes of faith. I never let go of the vision, no matter how hard it got.

MASTER THE POWER OF A POSITIVE MIND-SET WITH EVER INCREASING FAITH

When we have faith that we can do something, we can usually do it. If I go into the gym with someone and they are trying to bench press 300 lbs they are usually very confident and have faith they can do it. Maybe they did 290 lbs. the week before so they know they can do 300 lbs with a little more effort. Faith is just believing, even though you can't see it with your physical eyes. You must use your eyes of faith in order to see it.

I once heard a story about Jim Thorpe, who competed in the 1912 Summer Olympic Games in Stockholm. Jim pulled off one of the most impressive sporting feats in history, simply destroying the world's best score in the decathlon and pentathlon. He was unquestionably one of the greatest all-around athletes of all time, if not the greatest. But back in 1912 travel was much different than it is today. Athletes had to take a cruise ship in order to get to the 1912 Olympics.

While on the cruise ship all the athletes were practicing their events. But Jim Thorpe just sat there in a lounge chair and appeared to be working on his tan not his event. One of the other athletes came over and asked what he was doing and why he wasn't training. Jim said, "I am training. I am practicing the long jump. You see that line over there? Well, I am going over the long jump in my mind time and time again until I get it right." Jim Thorpe was an example of having faith and visualizing the result in advance. He used his eyes of faith to see his victory.

When I lift weights I can feel confident adding more weight to what I am lifting because I know what I did previously. When we have faith for our lives our faith increases every time we see things workout, so we have more faith for the future. With weights we may move up in 5 lb. increments or by adding another rep. With faith we take baby steps as well and get stronger in faith with every step. *With weight it is by the rep and with faith it is by the step.*

Listen, I am not here to preach at you. There are many people out there that are much better at it than I am. I am here to help you get the most out of your life and I am here to tell you that if you practice faith and choose a positive mind set, you will always be better off then if you dragged and moped around like you had the burden of the world resting on your shoulders. I know this from my own life and from the lives of many that I know. Faith is always better than faithlessness and positive is always better than negative.

When we are positive and full of faith our minds will change. Anything that happens on this earth starts in the mind. First we must believe it, and then we can achieve it. Only a fool would go after something that they thought was unachievable and I know your mama didn't raise no fool. As your faith increases, your positive mind set will follow and your actions will follow a positive mind set. If you truly believe you can do something then you will be unstoppable. How much could you achieve if you simply believed you couldn't fail?

THE WONDER OF WORDS AND SIMPLE GESTURES!

You can change your world by changing your words
... Remember, death and life are in the power of the tongue. —JOEL OSTEEN

Words have the power to build up or to tear down. They have the power to inspire and ignite the spirit or to extinguish a person's internal flame, the power to bless or to curse. Words can bring life to someone or death. The choice is yours. Choose to speak the words that will build up, inspire and ignite the spirit and bless those around you.

We all know someone that always wants to put someone else in their place. They usually do it with a sarcastic remark or quip. They use their words as a tool of destruction. Let's make a conscious decision right now not to put people in their place, but to lift them to a new place with your encouraging words. When you build up the people around you with your words, you will also lift yourself up. Be an encourager not a discourager, to yourself and to those around you.

WORDS CAN BRING LIFE!

I know a pastor who tells a story about a young lady that came into a church and sat on the back row. She just sat there by herself and when the service was over a member of the congregation went over and introduced himself to her, spent a few minutes getting to know her and let her know that she was noticed, wanted and welcome. In fact, he encouraged her to come back the following week. What he didn't know at the time was that she was going to kill herself that very day but had decided to go to church first. This man's encouragement changed this woman's life forever. Yes, there is power in your words and you will never know what impact they will have on those around you. It is amazing how you can lift people up with a little smile and with an encouraging word.

My wife, Cathy brings people to life with just a smile. It doesn't matter where we are. Cathy greets people with her beautiful smile and it brings them to life. We can be in a shopping center or on our way to the movies and Cathy has a smile for everyone and it changes those she sees every day. You can watch the posture of those she greets change and they leave her with a spring in their step and song in their heart and a smile on their face, all because Cathy took a moment to notice them and to greet them in love and joy.

In fact, that is how she won my heart. She was visiting her sister Sue in the hospital and I was visiting Sue's husband Andrew, who was my childhood friend. Sue had just given birth to their oldest son Drew. When Cathy entered the hospital room, she just greeted me with a smile. My heart jumped for joy and I heard a still small voice tell me "She will be your wife." My whole life changed for the better and forever with just a smile from the woman of my dreams. Sue also played match maker after this chance meeting to help fate along. Thanks Sue!

Decide today that you will have words of encouragement for the people you come in contact with. Give away a nice smile. Give a gift of joy to those you encounter and you will live a more joyful life. This is a free gift to others that is priceless. We can either infect our environment with a sour word and attitude or affect our environment with encouragement. Let's have an effect on our world. We live in a world in dire need of encouragement, so let it start with you and me today. You never know whose life you are affecting or saving with just a simple "Hello" and a smile.

The 1-2 Punch of Success...
Energy and Passion

The most essential factor is persistence - the determination never to allow your energy or enthusiasm (Passion) to be dampened by the discouragement that must inevitably come. —**James Whitcomb Riley**

When you have the energy to fuel your passion, success is sure to follow close behind. The 1-2 punch of energy and passion is the key to success in life. In order to be successful in any endeavor you will need to overcome much discouragement, frustration and failure and the key to rising above these things is energy and passion. That is why I always say that *energy is the fuel to ignite passion and passion is the engine of success!*

In the movie <u>Cinderella Man</u>, Russell Crowe plays a down and out boxer that makes a dramatic come back. The back drop to this movie is the great depression and previous to the great depression, Crowe's character, Jimmy Braddock, was a champion boxer that lost his way. After his come back a reporter asks him, *"You have lost before, what's the difference this time?"* Jimmy Braddock then answers, *"I know what I'm fighting for."* The reporter follows up with, *"And what's that?"* . Jimmy comes back with what I feel is the most memorable and inspiring line in the whole movie. He simply says, *"Milk."* That says it all. He now knew why he was fighting. He was fighting to feed his kids. He was able to look defeat straight in the face and say, "Okay, one more round." He was able to overcome failure because he had the energy and passion to achieve his goal of putting milk on the table. I feel this is the story of America. A spirit of passion for a worthy goal will let nothing stand in her way. *"Okay, let's go one more round."* was the unspoken mantra for generations of Americans and what has made America the greatest country in the world. Put the 1-2 punch of energy and passion to work in your life and live the life of your dreams.

GET EXCITED

Recently my wife and I had dinner with our friends Stu and Betsey Alexander and we started talking about our individual paths in life. Stu shared with us about how he started off in the U.S. Air Force Academy and how a tough officer changed his life with a few simple words.

Stu was into his senior year at the US Air Force Academy and ready to get out! Never enough sleep, constant pressure, unbelievable hours… Stu was simply burned out. One day, this all came to a head when giving an oral presentation. All seemed routine, when suddenly his instructor began dressing him down, big-time, in front of the class. Apparently, Stu had been a smart aleck in some of his responses……..and didn't even realize it. The instructor ate him alive right then and there, ordering him to his office after the class was over. When he got to the officer's office, Stu began to apologize. He explained that he didn't realize what he had done but clearly had offended him and others somehow. The Officer's response literally changed Stu's life forever.

He said, *"You know what you need, Cadet Alexander? You need something to get excited about."* Those words rang loud in Stu's head and he told me that the instructor was absolutely right. *"I did need something to get excited about! Something that would keep me going the rest of that year until graduation, something that would help me deal with everything else more effectively."* Stu said. Stu quickly thought about his instructor's advice and joined some other cadets and they put together a rock band.

Stu is quick to add that, *"It's all too easy to get bogged down in 'life': marriage, kids, job, career, mortgage, bills, investments, and yard work (ugh)………you name it. It's incredibly easy to reach that "burn out" point when juggling all these things. Trying to keep things going, can saturate anyone. We've all been there; those that haven't yet… will."* Stu then adds, *"Find something to get truly **excited** about. Better yet, don't wait until you are burned out. Find that thing or those things **now**."* By the way, Stu is still very passionate about his guitar and is the lead guitarist at his church. And if you ever spend any time with Stu, you will quickly find out that it still excites him! So take Stu's advice and go out and find something to get excited about!

THINK BIG

Hey, if you are going to think, why not think BIG! Little David didn't kill the giant Goliath by thinking small. Shah Jahan, didn't build one of the greatest monuments of all time, the Taj Mahal, by thinking small. Donald Trump didn't become "Donald Trump" by thinking small. Bill Gates didn't build Microsoft by thinking small and Arnold Schwarzenegger didn't become the Governor of California by accepting small thoughts. They all thought big and they expected more from themselves than anyone else could have possibly expected from them. They challenged themselves by going for grand expectations and not limiting their thoughts to the mundane and easy.

Jim Fraley, my track coach at Sewanhaka High School in New York used to tell me to shoot for the stars and if I don't make it, I would still land on the moon. So the worst thing that happens is you don't hit that big objective, but you are still better off and further along than if you were shooting for very little. Thinking small brings small results and thinking big brings big results.

Unfortunately, most people don't expect very much from themselves and because of this they are seldom disappointed. Is that you? Are you cheating yourself out of the best that life has for you and your family because you are afraid of disappointment? I have news for you. Deep down inside you are disappointed anyway, if you are not living up to your potential. The good news is this: you can change this in an instant by expecting more from yourself than anyone else would possibly expect. Look at the world and see what it has to offer you. Dig deep down inside yourself and try to remember those old childhood dreams you had. You know the ones. You had them long before anyone told you that achieving them was impossible. You used to think about them and the wonderful life you would have, back when nothing was impossible. Now write those dreams down and start nurturing them and then write a plan to achieve them. You are now on your way to living the life of your dreams. SO DREAM!!!!

THINKING **BIG** BRINGS OLYMPIAN SIZE RESULTS!

We all have dreams, some bigger than others. When I was in high school, I had the same coach that coached the great Olympian, Al Oerter, who won at four consecutive Olympics in the discus throw. Al would often come by, especially during the summer, to go to the open competitions with us kids. What a treat for us to get to spend some time with one of the greatest Olympic athletes of all time.

COACH FRALEY

Our coach often held team meetings and at one of these meetings, Coach Fraley asked the team why Al Oerter had won four consecutive Olympic gold medals, including some even when he was hurt. "How could he do it when he was injured so badly?" asked the coach. "He could barely move, but yet he WON?" He then called on me which he liked doing. I guess he found it entertaining to pick on me. I knew I could answer this one because Al Oerter was one of my hero's. I said, *"Because he wanted it so bad that he could taste it and was willing to put up with the pain to fulfill his goal."* Well, I got royally chewed out and publicly denigrated ... Fraley fashion. (I love Jim Fraley! He was tough on you, but had a great heart behind his toughness.) He told me, *"It was because he was well trained "you bull pimple!"* "Bull pimple" was a term of endearment from my tender coach. I recently contacted Al to ask him what the real answer was to this thirty year old question. I wanted to find out once and for all if I was indeed a "bull pimple". I asked Al, "Was *it training, true grit... or both?"* Al is a great man and champion. This was his response to the question I had been carrying with me for thirty years. *" I don't know if it was grit or training. All I can remember when walking out on the field in Tokyo, was that I was determined not to cheat myself out of four years of training. I honestly felt there was some capability still inside, regardless of how much pain I was bombarded with. I did train for 365 days a year throwing as hard as I possibly could in every throwing session. I just flat out knew myself and could not bag it."* Al not only thought big, but he trained big and expected more from himself than anyone else would have possibly expected. If he had walked off the field of competition injured, no one would have blamed him or thought less of him. He had already won two other consecutive gold medals in two previous Olympics before he was seriously injured during the 1964 Olympic Games in Tokyo.

The bottom line is, Al Oerter would not settle for anything less from himself but his best effort. He simply would not "bag it". He was shooting for the stars and if he landed on the moon, at least he shot for the stars. If he lost he could at least look back and say that he gave it his best. History now shows that Al Oerter, from the United States, won the discus throw and broke his own Olympic record, despite a cervical disc injury that forced him to wear a neck harness and a torn rib cartilage, that he incurred a week before the competition. Today, Al is a highly acclaimed artist and is currently traveling around the country with *Art of the Olympians,* which includes fourteen Olympian artists from seven countries. Al is now conquering the art world and continues to think big. That is one of the reasons that Al Oerter has always been and will always be one of my hero's. He never did let me know if I was a "bull pimple", though. He is a gentleman and maybe I don't need to know. Some things are best left unknown.

FORGET YESTERDAY
FOR BETTER RESULTS TOMORROW

The following story is from my good friend, Dottie Walters. She is a wonderful example of many of the principles in this book. See if you can find a few. One is the fact that she didn't let her devastating yesterday dictate her extraordinary future. Dottie Walters, CSP, is the President of *The Walters International Speakers Bureau* and has a list of credentials too long to mention. She is quite simply a legend in the professional speaking industry and I am blessed to call her my friend. Let's listen to Dottie as she tells us a little about herself and gives us some wonderful advice on life in her own words. *(Note: It grieves me to put this note in. My friend Dottie Walters went home to be with the Lord on February 14, 2007. She is finally reunited with her sweetheart Robert Emmett Walters.)*

JOHN WITH DOTTIE WALTERS
DECEMBER 31, 1924 - FEBRUARY 14, 2007

"My father and mother were divorced when I was on the brink of starting high school. He was a cruel man, who insisted on using a sharp stick to hit my fingers with as he grilled me on arithmetic. However, my mother took me to the Public Library every week - I started going before I could read. The librarian showed me the children's books that were in series, and I fell in love with reading the whole group of those books, then looking for more.

Just as my father was leaving my mother and I, she asked him on our front porch where all of our neighbors could hear them, "What about Dorothy going to college?" He answered her in a very loud voice, "She is too DUMB to ever be allowed to attend any college."

I took many different jobs during this period to help my mother, and I learned a lot about different kinds of bosses as I worked.

I told my librarian friend about how excited I was to be moving on up to high school. She took me to a room I had not seen before. She explained that this was the room where they kept the books about "People of Achievement." Then she pointed to a book right by my hand and told me, "Start here – and read every book in this room." That first book was the "Autobiography of

Benjamin Franklin!" I soon learned that I heard the voices of all of those wonderful "People of Achievement" in their books!

My high school English teacher asked each member of her class to write a story based on one of the characters from Charles Dickens "A Tale of Two Cities." She read mine aloud to the class! My heart was floating around the room. Then she said that I would be the Advertising Manager and Feature Editor of our Alhambra High School newspaper! That same wonderful day she told me I must get my first editorials and features ready for her by the next morning.

My job was at a bakery built inside a grocery store - "MacDaniels Midnight Market." When I had all the glass cases and the floors scrubbed, my job was to dump the trash in the big dumpster at the back of the market. But I was worried because I had no paper to write the items my teacher had asked me for, for our school newspaper. As I carried out the trash, I noticed that the soiled bakery bags were only sticky on one side! I tore off the sticky parts and soon had a nice stack of clean paper. The market was very quiet in the later part of the evening, so I was able to write all the items my teacher had asked for the Alhambra High Moor Newspaper! I can still hear her laughing the next morning when she saw the paper I had used!

My sweetheart joined the United States Marine Corps when Pearl Harbor was bombed. He fought in all of the battles of the South Pacific. He was gone for four years, but we wrote to each other every day for four years.

As I began my advertising business later to help with our family expenses, he always helped me with the children and with encouragement. Bob died two years ago—we all miss him very much, but feel his loving spirit always close to us.

Today, my company publishes an international speaker's magazine called "Sharing Ideas" and we operate a speakers bureau, sending professional paid speakers all over the world. I also consult with many speakers who want to move up in the speaking and writing business.

I have spoken all over the world myself. My advice to your readers is to think as my Scottish Grandpa did. Put your fingers on the pulse just below your thumb and repeat what he told me - "We may be knocked down many times, but we NEVER STAY DOWN!"

Well Dottie's Grandpa was right. *"We may be knocked down many times, but we NEVER STAY DOWN!"*

Getting knocked down may be out of your control but staying down.....now, that is something you are in complete control of. If you haven't already gotten up, then do it now. It is never too late. I know people who were abused by a parent in such a way that should never happen to a child. It could have broken them, but instead they went on to be incredibly successful in life. We have absolutely no way to change the past. All we can do is forgive the person or people and get on with our future.

From Victim to Victor

Many people use yesterday as an excuse for doing nothing today. They are a victim to their past. Well if that is you, it is time to go from victim to victor. Everyone likes the boxer that picks himself off the mat to win the fight. We all love the Rocky movies because Sylvester Stallone has taken Rocky and made him our friend, a friend that knows how to face adversity and win.

No one wants to keep hearing your sob story. The only one you are hurting by lamenting on your past is yourself. People love underdogs that rise up from the ashes to conquer the world, but no one wants to continually hear your woes. Today is a new day. Do you have something to overcome in order to live the life of your dreams? Well stop holding yourself back by telling yourself and everyone else what happened yesterday and just start living successfully today. The fact of the matter is that no one wants to hear about your woes anyway. Yes, maybe once or twice, but after awhile it gets old. People respect and are inspired by the person who can pick themselves up from *their* mat and go one more round. Win or lose, that person is victorious.

If we focus on the past, we simply will not attack our future with passion. If yesterday knocked you down, get up, brush yourself off and get on to tomorrow with a passion and a determination that will set you apart from the crowd. Then the world will stand up, cheer and take notice!

THE PHYSIOLOGY OF SUCCESS...
EMOTION FOLLOWS MOTION!

Have you ever had a day when you were totally exhausted? All you wanted to do was sit down and rest? Then all of a sudden you had to do something physically challenging and you woke up and even got energized? I try not to workout in the evenings for this very reason. If I go to the gym too late at night, I can't get to sleep. Do you go to a ball game very tired and then your team scores and you jump up and start cheering and all of a sudden you are alive and vibrant again? That is because our body can jump start our energy.

I want you to take a moment right now and stand up. That's right, stop what you are doing and stand up. No one is looking at you, so get up. Now look down at the floor, slump your shoulders and stand like you do when you are exhausted. See how tired and weak you feel? Once you are totally exhausted I want to show you how easy it is to feel strong. Now look up, get a great big smile on your face and do a "power move". Throw a punch and say, "Yeah! " or do some kind of energetic move and make a powerful sound. Take deep breaths and feel fully alive. Do you see the difference in how you feel? Do you feel more energetic, more alive and stronger? Athletes do things like this all the time to get "psyched up" to do what they have to do. Your life is no less important than the athletic event the athlete is getting "psyched up" for, is it? This goes to show you that emotion follows motion!

You can see this at a concert, at a sporting event or even at church. If you are sitting there and just watching the event, you get a little bored and listless, but the moment you get up and start cheering your physical energy begins to pick up. At my church, we do about a half hour of praise and worship music before the pastor begins to speak. When the songs are slow you can see the energy of the congregation sag a little, but as soon as an up-beat song is playing and everyone begins to move a little, you can see the energy in the whole building begin to build. This is the physiology of success with the help of music. And by the way, music is a great accompaniment to getting yourself up out of a slump. Put some up-beat music on, move yourself in a powerful and energetic way and before long you will be powerful and energetic, too.

Action Steps

Remember, the world doesn't reward us for what we know;
it rewards us for what we do!

1. Get enthusiastic.
2. Fill your mind with thoughts that support you.
3. Believe in yourself and know that you are here for a reason.
4. Have faith in yourself.
5. Control your tongue. Speak words that bring life.
6. Combine your energy with passion for lifelong success. Remember, energy is the fuel to ignite passion and passion is the engine of success!
7. Think big and get excited about life.
8. Look toward a bright tomorrow, even if yesterday was cloudy.
9. Move powerfully, remember emotion follows motion.

CHAPTER

$$\boxed{4}$$

Purpose... Know Your "Why"

THE POWER OF PURPOSE

Many people have a wrong idea of what constitutes true happiness.
It is not attained through self-gratification, but through fidelity to a worthy purpose.
—HELEN KELLER

I believe that each of us is born with a destiny, an undeniable purpose for our life. Recognizing and honoring this purpose is probably one of the hallmarks of successful people. They take enough interest in their own lives to examine "why" they are here and what they are meant to do. Then they do it and do it with passion, enthusiasm and abandon.

Find your "WHY"

Knowing why you are doing something is often as important as how to do it. In fact, if you don't know why, you will not stick to it. If you have a big enough why, the how will take care of itself because you will search heaven and earth until you know how.

Knowing your why will motivate you and help you overcome the obstacles that are sure to come. Knowing and defining your why will also help you with your goal setting. For example, if you are trying to get into shape, some people use an upcoming school or family reunion as their "why". Some use business objectives and yet for others it is a spiritual pursuit to define their "why". I know many people that constantly have an upcoming "why". An example is a good friend of mine that stays in great shape. He breaks the year up into events to train for. First, he starts off with the summer and looking good and performing well as a life guard at the beach. Then his new goal will be a party that is coming up in October. His next goal might be seeing people at the holidays and wanting to look his best. Then it is a ball or some type of event that happens in the spring and wanting to look fit for those. Before you know it, we are back to summer again. I know that a lot of my friends at church will tell me that this is vain and not very humble. Zig Ziglar has said that being humble is not thinking less of yourself, but thinking of yourself less. By setting these short-term goals, they will help you focus on the things that may be a little harder but will give the motivation to stick to plan anyway. These are not egotistical goals my friend sets, they are just milestones to help him keep himself motivated.

Without your why… without your life's purpose, it is so easy to get side-tracked and distracted in life and do busy work, while getting nothing accomplished toward your purpose for being here. Just going through the motions of life can be exhausting, but find your purpose and you will be "living in the zone". The zone is where you find effortless energy.

LIVING IN THE ZONE!

Find your purpose and BANG you're in the zone! Life just works. It all comes together. Living on purpose means doing what you love, doing what you are passionate about, and doing what you are good at. In other words, you are in the zone! I remember many years ago someone told me that if I took my hobby and made it my vocation that I would not only be rich but incredibly happy. No truer words were ever spoken and there is a reason for this. The things we are good at, passionate about and love doing are part of our make up. It is part of who we are and why we are here. Not only will you be more fulfilled but the world will benefit from your passions. It is incredible, because when you are living in the zone, all the things you need will naturally gravitate towards you. I think it is because you are benefiting others through your life's work.

You see this with athletes. When Michael Jordan is just effortlessly performing on the basketball court, he is having a great time. He looks like he is putting in very little effort, but no one can touch him…he is in the zone. How about Tiger Woods? He looks like he is just taking a walk in the park and gently hitting the golf ball totally relaxed but the ball goes screaming down the fare way at a tune of over 300 yards, straight as an arrow heading directly at the pin. It is pure poetry in motion. The zone, Baby,…pure zone. It doesn't mean Michael and Tiger don't work hard at what they do. They work harder than most, but what they do is their passion. What is the zone for you? What do you do with very little effort that others struggle to accomplish or simply can't accomplish and yet for you it is natural and easy? Find your zone and you have found your purpose.

> *Everything--a horse, a vine--is created for some duty…For what task, then, were*
> *you yourself created? A man's true delight is to do the things he was made for.*
> **—MARCUS AURELIUS**

Do you want to live a delightful life? Man, I think we all do! I love the sound of that… a delightful life. It is almost musical. That Marcus Aurelius was really a *"good talker"*. That is what they said in the *"neighborhood"* when I was a kid. If you were well spoken and articulate…Oh, then you where a REAL good talker. It sounds better if you insert a Brooklyn accent, so come out to one of my seminars and hear me speak and you will really hear a "good talker", a REAL good talker with an authentic accent. Okay, let's get back on *purpose* here.

Knowing why you are here is probably the most energizing revelation you can have. You can be a bundle of energy, but if you don't know what you are supposed to do with your life, you can short circuit your life and in the process feel exhausted. Have you ever had a day when you knew exactly what to do and you felt great and the day flew by? The reverse is also true. We have all had days where we didn't have a clue of what we were supposed to do, if anything and we felt tired, frustrated and the day dragged by. Knowing our purpose in life keeps us energized and on target with our lives.

BE CLEAR WHY YOU ARE HERE

Decide upon your major definite purpose in life and then organize all your activities around it. —BRIAN TRACY

If you are clear on why you are here, organizing your daily activities becomes easier. Everything you do will be geared toward fulfilling your life's purpose. If you are doing something and it is not in line with why you are here, you will simply not do it. Period.

Get rid of the busy work from your life. Stop getting busy with busy work, stop getting-ready-to-get-ready. Get going on what you are gifted at and focus on the end result.

DISCOVERING THE CHAMPION IN YOU

All my life, I watched as people succeeded in sports, in business and in their family. What was it that made them so good? What made them so much better than everyone else? Well, there are a lot of factors, but one very important factor was that they loved what they were doing and were doing what they loved.

The athlete that gets to bed early so he can get up early to practice is doing it out of love for the sport. The business person that betters himself or herself by reading and continuing to grow is doing it out of a passion for excellence in his or her career and life. The mom or dad that sits at the bedside of their child praying along with the innocent hopeful prayers of a child, when they have a hundred other things to do, does it because this moment is much more valuable to them than all the other things that are pulling at them.

You can see it in the face of the athlete, the business person and the parent. There is a joy and a peace that goes along with doing what you know you should be doing and doing what you are here to do. The opposite is also true. When people are forcing their lives to workout, it is always evident. Life just doesn't flow for them and that is felt by everyone around them.

FOCUS ON YOUR STRENGTHS

As John Maxwell said in an article entitled personal growth, *"Choose to grow in the areas of your strengths, not in the areas of your weakness. There are only four things I do well, just four, and I focus exclusively on them. I lead, communicate, create, and network. That's it. I spend all of my time on one of those four strength zones. The secret of successful people lies in their ability to discover their strengths and to organize their lives so that these strengths can be applied."* John Maxwell gives us excellent advice here. If we are focusing on our weakness, then we just develop our weakness and never achieve greatness. Greatness doesn't come from focusing on your weaknesses, mediocrity does. Greatness lies in focusing on and strengthening your strengths, because that is where your gift lies.

In my own life, I have a few things that I am outstanding at and many that I am weak at. For many years I thought I had to focus on my weaknesses, so I could get better at them and be more well-rounded. But what happened was that I just got mediocre in those areas and neglected my areas of strength; losing out on both ends. I am not saying that you shouldn't try to get better in things you are no good at. What I am saying is, you should spend the majority of your time operating in your gifting and you will achieve outstanding success. The added bonus to this is that you will enjoy your life much more. When I am operating in areas I am strong and knowledgeable in, the day flies by and I get a lot accomplished. When I am operating in areas where I am limited and weaker, I flounder and the day drags.

GREATNESS SOMETIMES MEANS GOING AGAINST THE GRAIN

Unfortunately for many of us, focusing on our weaknesses is taught to us in school and at home. I remember one time coming home with a hand full of gold medals from a large track meet and when I entered the door to my house, I was beaming with excitement to show my parents how well I had done. The response I got was, *"You should only do so good in school"*. This was meant to spur me on in school. I think this mindset is very common in our society, but common isn't what changes the world. Many people are threatened by achievers, so they criticize what they are uncomfortable with. The rewards go to the achievers... the uncommon... and that is a very important distinction. You will encounter resistance from family, friends or people at work. It just comes with the territory. You will need to be careful of those from whom you are getting your accolades, they just may be holding you back. Even if you are the best of the mediocre, you are still mediocre! Do as Oprah Winfrey says, *"Surround yourself with only people who are going to lift you higher."* It seems to have worked for Oprah. I know it will work for you.

I LEARNED HOW TO FOCUS ON MY STRENGTHS OUT OF DESPERATION *NOT* INSPIRATION!

When I went into Manhattan real estate, I couldn't read a financial statement and I thought taking the minutes of a corporate meeting was literally timing the meeting. My very first day at work, I had a board of directors meeting at 7 Park Avenue and I was asked to do the minutes. The next morning my boss, Mark Harris, asked me publicly if I did the minutes for 7 Park Ave. and I exuberantly shouted across our Madison Avenue office, *"Yes sir, Mr. Harris. It took exactly 128 minutes!"* He just laughed and told everyone in the office that I was such a card and asked that I have the minutes on his desk within an hour.

My secretary, Linda, came blasting into my office and slammed the door. *"You don't even know what minutes are...DO YOU!"* she exclaimed. *"Calm down."* I said, *"Based on your rosy attitude, I am assuming it isn't timing the meeting, is it?"* *"Well no."* she said in a huff. *"Ok, well let me know what they are and we will get them done."* I was trying hard to stay cool, but I was sweating! It seemed like just the day before I was in a janitor's closet and today, I had my own office on Madison Ave.! She then explained that the minutes were the corporate records of the meeting and then she threw in that she wasn't going to lose her job because of me. I then told her that if she helped me keep my job for the first year, she wouldn't regret it. "After all," I told her, "if I get fired, you would have to work with one of the boring guys in this the office that knows how to do everything. I can guarantee working with me will not be boring or dull!" I said with an impish smile. Linda was incredible and I wouldn't have made it through my first year without her!

After this experience, I realized that I wasn't going to excel on Madison Avenue based on my knowledge of the corporate world or my good looks, so I took a different route. All of my co-workers were older than me and had many years of corporate experience. Among my experiences...I was...well...a janitor and in this field I'd learned not only about cleaners and cleaning, but had training in boilers, refrigeration, structural maintenance and grounds maintenance. No one thought I would make it through my first week…except me! It kind of juiced me up. It was a challenge and I was up for it. I quickly decided that if I was going to stay on Madison Avenue, I had to be different so I focused on my strengths. My strengths were networking, my understanding of the physical aspect of buildings, my ability to speak to my building maintenance staff as easily as I could speak in the board room (Did I mention that I was a REAL GOOD TALKER?) and, of course, my ambition. I also expected success. Failure wasn't an option. Oh, did I mention that I was very ambitious and expected to succeed! That is very important. *I focused on success and what tools I had, as opposed to being afraid of failure and focusing on what I didn't have.* You need to read that again until it sinks in because it is profound, if I do say so myself. I will always point out to you when I am being profound so you won't miss it.

With all of this in mind, I set out to get to know everyone and anyone in the real estate industry that was powerful and influential. I went after the best of the best and many of them are still friends of mine today. I quickly set myself apart from the other managers. Sure they could read a financial statement, but I could make the noticeable improvements in a building that everyone could see and I did. I went into these buildings at midnight and trained my staff. In fact, I became known for putting on my work clothes and working WITH them when necessary. They had never seen this before. The only time the staff saw the property manager was when the manager was walking around in his $2,000.00 suit and Rolex, not dressed in work clothes and working hand-in-hand with the staff. When the residents got up in the morning, the brass was shining, the marble was glowing and the staff was buzzing about this new *"crazy---but cool"* manager.

I also got to know every superintendent in Manhattan and won over all of my Board of Directors. In short, within months I was very well known and highly respected. I was offered a huge raise to go to another company, which I took. I certainly wasn't the best manager, but I was different. I stood out and excelled because I focused on my strengths. I also knew where I was going…and it wasn't back to Brooklyn!

Where would you like to go?

I am sure you don't have your work cut out for you the way I did….. or maybe you do. Either way, a good part of success comes from deciding what you want and expecting to get it. What you expect is what you will get. If you are expecting failure and defeat, your subconscious mind will work with you to make sure you aren't disappointed. But if you are expecting success and victory, your subconscious mind will work with you there as well. It will support you and have you doing the things that will bring these positive things into your life. You will get what you focus on. If you are constantly focusing on the negative, you will live a negative life but, if you fill your mind with the positive, you will live a positive life. Decide where you want to go and expect to get there. Constantly tell yourself that is where you are going.

Get your hopes up! Faith is the things <u>hoped</u> for and can't be seen. The faith that we will have an incredible future comes out of hope for a better future even though we can't see it. Have faith and be hopeful, great things are in store for you! But it all starts with hope and expecting and seeing the unsee-able!

ENLARGE YOUR VISION

My mother said to me, "If you become a soldier, you'll be a general;
if you become a monk, you'll end up as the Pope." Instead, I became a painter
and wound up as Picasso. —PABLO PICASSO

Boy oh boy, it doesn't sound like Picasso had a self esteem problem. How could he, with such an encourager for a mother? He knew he could go far because he was taught by his mother that greatness was inside of him. Let me tell you right now that the seed of greatness is inside of you as well. You just need to water it with hope, faith and belief and it will bloom into a life beyond your dreams.

Until 1954, it was thought impossible to break four minutes running the mile. Experts of the day said everything from, "Man's legs can't move that fast for that long" to "The human heart would explode under such strain." But on May 6, 1954, in a meet at Oxford in England, as Roger Bannister broke the tape and collapsed, the announcer delivered his time for the mile run to the cheering crowd; 3 minutes, 59.4 seconds. The unbreakable record had been broken. Roger Bannister had made history. Then 46 days later, John Landy duplicated Bannister's feat, breaking the world record in the process. Within 10 years, 336 runners broke that barrier. Today, even high school runners break the four minute mile. I guess the experts were wrong. Well, yes and no.

Yes, the experts were wrong that the human body couldn't do it because Bannister showed that the body can. But NO, the experts weren't wrong as long as we believed the experts! As soon as one man enlarged his vision, he opened the flood gates of opportunity to others. You will never go beyond your own self imposed barriers. If you think you can do it, you are right and if you think you can't do it, you are also right.

Do you have a four minute mile in your own life? A barrier that needs to be overcome? Are you stuck in poverty because your family has always been poor? Do you have addictions like your parents and grandparents? Are you sick and you just expect to be sick because everyone in your family is sick a lot? Are you a hot head with a terribly destructive temper like your mom or dad? Are you an abusive spouse or parent, but you have no choice because you were abused as a child? STOP and STOP RIGHT NOW!!! Those are nothing but four-minute miles in your life. They are self imposed prison bars and the only way to get out of jail is to change your own thinking. Enlarge your vision and expect more for your life. You were created for a grand purpose, now stop letting the four minute miles in your life stop you. Look beyond the obstacles to the finish line and run the good race. Today is your day. It is the day that was made just for you and what a beautiful day it is!

DO YOU FORGET TO REMEMBER?

There is a miracle in your head. You have had successes and experiences that have touched and shaped you in a way that is undeniable. You know about it, but do you remember it on a regular basis? It is so much more natural to focus on our hardships and problems than it is to remember the victories and successes, but the power is in remembering the ladder.

Remember the time you got the promotion over someone more qualified? Remember the time you saw the face of the person that would bless your life beyond belief, that person that would become your spouse? Remember the birth of your children? Remember the victory over depression, addiction, financial hardship or just plain stinking thinking? Remember the good, great and victorious times in your life. Remembering these things, will lift your spirits to new heights and super charge your future so you can become the person you were created to be!

Remembering and focusing on your victories and successes will put you in an attitude of gratitude and that is where you will flourish. You can do so much more when you are thankful. The power of living a grateful life carries over into your attitude and behavior towards your future and towards others.

When we remember the good, the positive and the uplifting, we know we can do more of the same. We are over comers. We are conquerors. But we were created to be more than conquerors. To be a conqueror is incredible, but to be more than a conqueror means that nothing is out of reach. We can be victors as opposed to victims. A victorious attitude comes across to others as well. Everyone likes to be around an upbeat, positive person and most want to avoid the Eeyores of this world. You know what I am talking about. Eeyore. The donkey that hung around Winnie the Pooh.

Eeyore, the old grey donkey, stood by the side of the stream, and looked at himself in the water. "Pathetic," he said, "That's what it is. Pathetic." He turned and walked slowly down the stream for twenty yards and splashed across it, and walked slowly back on the other side. Then he looked at himself in the water. "As I thought," he said. "No better from this side. But nobody minds. Nobody cares. Pathetic, that's what it is." —WINNIE THE POOH

This is pathetic! When you act like that, you don't even want to be around yourself, so why would others. Success comes out of faith not fear! Remembering the victories of the past puts more faith in your present and future.

YOU ARE HERE FOR A REASON

This is very important to consider. There is only one you and the gifts that are inside of you are there to serve me and the rest of the world. When we don't know our "why" and don't operate in our unique genius, we are depriving the world of the gift that we are. In other words we are depriving the world of our unique contribution and to me that seems incredibly selfish.

YOU, yes you. You are a blessing to the world. The only one of your kind ever created. You are priceless. So start acting that way.

Action Steps

Remember, the world doesn't reward us for what we know;
it rewards us for what we do!

1. Find your purpose in life and go for it with abandon.
2. Focus on your strengths and giftings.
3. Determine where you are going.
4. Enlarge your vision.
5. Write down a list of past successes to remind you when times are tough. Don't forget to remember.
6. Remember that you are here for a reason. You are a gift to the world.

CHAPTER

5

Your Road Map to Success

My philosophy of life is that if we make up our mind what we are going to make of

our lives, then work hard toward that goal, we never lose - somehow we win out.

—RONALD REAGAN

The world seems to just workout when a person knows what his goals in life are. A goal is a success magnet. Once you set a goal worthy of your life, you will some how be pulled toward that objective. People, circumstances and events will all seem to be working for you and for your good.

UNLEASH THE POWER OF GOALS

Your goals are the road maps that guide you and show you

what is possible for your life. —LES BROWN

Goals are the road map to your future. Walking through life with no goals is like driving across country with no road map. You will get somewhere, but it may not be where you wanted to go. Set your path with goals and see your dreams come true. Yogi Berra, the famous Yankee, put it this way, *"You've got to be very careful if you don't know where you are going, because you might not get there."* That Yogi sure had a way with words, didn't he? He was quite the talker!

> *If you're bored with life -- you don't get up every morning*
> *with a burning desire to do things -- you don't have enough goals.*
> —LOU HOLTZ

KNOW WHAT YOU WANT

Life with me has never been boring. Just ask my wife, as soon as I achieve one goal, I am on to the next. I am always pursuing the next goal and with this comes never ending growth and self improvement. It keeps me pumped up, alive, full of energy and excited about life. *Robert Schuller* hit the nail on the head when he said, *"Goals are not only absolutely necessary to motivate us. They are essential to really keeping us alive."* So if you want to feel alive, set empowering goals!

FROM BOILER ROOM TO BOARD ROOM

The fuel of a goal brought me from the basement of a boiler room in Brooklyn, to a board room on Madison Avenue. I literally had to work my way out of the basement. Goals then propelled me from the board room on Madison Ave to owning the "East Coast Mecca of Bodybuilding", the gym I dreamed of owning as a child. I knew exactly where I was going even though others thought I would fail. The fact of the matter is, that I was willing to fail if that is what it took for me to reach my goals. Like Og Mandino said, *"Failure will never overtake me if my determination to succeed is strong enough."*

What you achieve in setting goals is incredible and the only thing that overshadows your achievements is what you become. Zig Ziglar is absolutely right when he says, *"What you get by achieving your goals is not as important as what you become by achieving your goals."* Goals are life changing and as you achieve your goals you are transformed as well.

It doesn't matter where you are coming from. All that matters is where you are going.

—BRIAN TRACY

Come on! Let's design your perfect future.

You can download goal setting forms at www.JohnMRowley.com/bookbonus

HOW TO SET GOALS:

Action Step 1:

List all of your goals and next to it the time line in which you would like them completed. i.e. within 1, 3, 5, 10, 20 years.

_____

_____

_____

_____

_____

_____

_____

_____

_____

_____

_____

_____

_____

_____

_____

Action Step 2:

Write down "why" next to all of the things on your list and write a paragraph why you are committed to achieving it. "Why" is very powerful.

_____

_____

_____

_____

_____

_____

_____

_____

_____

Action Step 3:

Divide your goals into three categories: Short range (1 month or less), Mid range (1 month to 1 year) and Long range (1 year or more) goals.

_____

_____

_____

_____

_____

_____

_____

_____

_____

Action Step 4:

For each of your top 5 goals write down one action you can do today to get started.

The important thing is to start today and adjust your goals as needed.

_____

_____

_____

_____

_____

_____

_____

_____

_____

_____

SUCCESS MODELING

I wasn't the best athlete in the world or the sharpest guy on Madison Avenue. But I knew how to find them. Whether it was as an athlete or business person, I would seek out the best and find out what made them tick.

When I was in high school, I worked for my father during the summer and holidays to earn extra money. I learned an incredible work ethic being around my father, which has helped me all of my life. He was not much in the way of giving verbal advice, but I sure learned a lot just being around him. He had and still has incredible integrity and a great work ethic. My father ran a New York City School and would hire extra help every summer to do all the maintenance things that could not be done during the school year. Some of this extra summer help would be top runners from the New York area. We would work all morning, then at lunch time we would run stairs or do wind sprints in the hallways or go outside and do speed work. This is how I learned how to model people. I would saddle up to these guys, work hand in hand with them and get into their heads to see what made them tick. They were thrilled to make the extra money and we all enjoyed being around these other great runners.

One summer, a great 400 meter guy worked with us. His name was Anthony Tufferilo. "Tuffy", as he was called, was the best 400-meter runner in the country.

His dad was an electrician for the board of education and a friend of my dad's. My dad knew that I would learn a lot by being around Tuffy all summer, so he hired him and we became fast friends. (pun intended)

One day, we went to a track to do 200-meter intervals. When we were running, Tuffy told me to go at about 80% effort. He said it was a good exercise in control. I said, "Come on 80% is not hard enough." Tuffy told me that if you can go 80%, you will be going faster than you think because you will be relaxed. Basically, running at 80% has you running fast, but not pushing with intensity and it keeps your mind relaxed, which in turn relaxes your body. It teaches you to be relaxed while running. Tuffy was the most controlled and relaxed runner I have ever seen and also the fastest. Later that year he went on to win the *Golden West*; the most prestigious High School meet in the country which was held in California. He then went to Villanova on a full scholarship. I didn't follow his college career but I know he was shooting for the 1980 Olympics which were cancelled because of the Iran hostage crisis. I am sure he is successful with whatever he is doing. The 80% lesson carried me into the business world, as I found my pace and strove to keep the fire in my belly under control, so I would not burn out with all the long hours that I worked.

It also taught me that I can learn a lot from others and save years on the learning curve. Why reinvent the wheel when you can learn from someone else? Plus if you are putting out 80% in the work place, you are putting out about 70% more than 80% of your competitors. The other 20% are excelling and they are the ones to learn from.

In the business world, I have had many mentors. One of them is Barbara Corcoran. Barbara started her own real estate company with no more than a dream and the $1,000.00 she had borrowed. She turned that into the largest real estate brokerage company in Manhattan.

Barbara had lived in one of the buildings I'd managed and we met by chance. She was doing a renovation in her apartment and she needed some assistance from me. During this process, we got to know each other and developed a lifelong friendship. Barbara was very busy, but never too busy to return a call or to meet me for breakfast to help and guide me. In fact, many years later when I needed a job, she hired me as a broker. The first thing she told me to do was to get to know Dan Douglas and Jeff Levitas, two of the top brokers in Manhattan. She knew that I would be more successful much faster if I could learn what Dan and Jeff did and do the same thing. So that is what I did. Today Dan, Jeff and I are still friends. Dan and Jeff are still some of the best brokers in Manhattan working for the Corcoran Group.

Outstanding people will show you what they did to be successful. It is very simple.

1. Find someone who's already getting the results that you want.
2. Find out what that person is doing.
3. Do the same things and you will get the same results.

I have always tried to surround myself with the most successful people I could find. Success leaves clues and I am a success detective. A byproduct of seeking out success models is that you end up with life long friends that have the same passions that you have and then you end up helping each other over the years. This is a two way street and you should always give more than you receive.

Finding people to model is just a matter of looking for people that are successful in the area you are focusing on. I find that if I ask someone if I can sit with them and find out what makes them successful, they are usually complimented by my asking. In fact, in over 25 years of doing this, no one has ever turned me down. People that are in great shape or successful in other areas of their life, love it when someone notices and tells them. They also love to share the secrets of their success. The truth is that most people don't ask and are not interested.

When I worked in Manhattan, I made it a point to have lunch with someone successful once a week. I would call the movers and the shakers in the Manhattan real estate market and tell them that I wanted to get to know them and to see what made them tick, so I could emulate their success. I never had anyone turn me down. I built an incredible network this way, besides all the learning I did.

Get curious and find people to model. Then become a person worth modeling so you can give back. In fact, sometimes you learn more by teaching.

THE POWER OF HABITS

You become what you do all the time. We all have habits, some good, and some bad. We get up on the same side of the bed, dress ourselves and brush our teeth the same way every day. If you have empowering habits, you will be more successful in life. If you have habits that limit you, replace them with habits that support your goals.

Are Your Habits Helpful or Hurtful?

It is up to you. Develop your helpful habits now so they can kick in when you encounter Gravity. Gravity is automatic and it's everywhere. You don't need to try much for gravity to take over. You want to fall on your face, gravity is there to help. You want to fall down the stairs, gravity is there. You want to fall off a roof, again gravity is there. Do you want to climb to the heights of success, face overcoming odds and succeed time and time again? Do you want to start a new business, become the best in your current business, lose weight, become financially independent? You don't have to look too hard to find gravity, it is pulling at you as you try to succeed. People help gravity by telling you things like, "You can't do that. That won't work. Why bother?" Your habits are your anti-gravity suite in life. They pull you up to success.

It takes effort to be successful and to fight against the natural tendency of gravity, which is, of course, to pull you down to the ground. It is nothing personal. Gravity doesn't get mad. It just does its job. Your job is to fight gravity and any of the tools it uses to keep you down. You are in control of your destiny. You can lose weight if you want to. You can add muscle to your body. You can be more vibrant, have the energy that is required to fight gravity and become successful at the goals you have always wanted to achieve both in business and in your personal life. In fact, the more you fight gravity, the stronger you become and the stronger you become, the less effect gravity will have on you. You can become the person you know you should be! It is up to you to develop the habits necessary for your success in all areas of your life.

How to develop new and empowering habits:

Developing new habits takes time. The rule of thumb is that it takes 21 days to develop a new habit. This is probably true for small habits, but for large lifestyle changes I want you to be persistent and patient. True lifestyle changes may take longer.

Imagine if you exchanged two limiting habits for two empowering habits every year. In five years, that would be ten empowering habits that you do without effort. That is with only two a year. What if you did six a year? In five years, you would have thirty empowering habits. Do you think your life would be different with thirty empowering habits? All your successes would pile up on top of each other and you would have an extraordinary quality of life by making these small daily changes.

In order to change your habits:

1. You must define them, so write down all the habits that limit you.
2. Define your new successful habit in detail. Write down what you will do in place of your old, limiting habits.
3. Develop an action plan for this new habit.

This may be as simple as scheduling time to exercise or researching a new business opportunity. Keep it as simple as possible. Make it easy to be successful in all areas of your life.

Master your habits or they WILL master you!

Take Action!

The great end of life is not knowledge but action.
—**Thomas Huxley**

The world doesn't reward us for what we know; it rewards us for what we do. For those that are in control of their own destiny, action is the key. We all know people that appear to have great knowledge, but never do anything with their lives. We all know that person that prides him or herself on being an "academic". Being the person that knows absolutely everything about everything… your basic "know-it-all". He or she is very quick to offer unsolicited advice to anyone who will listen and often to those who don't want to listen. Whenever I speak to a person like this, I am quickly reminded of what Albert Einstein once said, *"Information is not knowledge."* The sad thing is that often, people like this seldom achieve anything with all the information they say they have.

People like this should listened to what Richard Keeves has to say, *"Knowledge might be power, but only when you take action."* The key is to DO something, not to just talk about it. If you have an outstanding education, that is a great and wonderful asset. The key is to use it. Put your knowledge to work on the streets, in the board room and in the business world. Don't just use it while sitting on your couch, watching the TV game show Jeopardy, trying to impress your family and friends so you can become a legend in your own mind.

Everything you want is out there waiting for you to ask. Everything you want also wants you. But you have to take action to get it. —Jack Canfield

Success in life isn't easy, but it is simple. Jack Canfield hit the nail right on the head. Just take massive action every day until you achieve the life of your dreams. When you try something and it doesn't work, change your strategy. Living the life of your dreams puts you in the captain's seat. The captain of a plane knows he will be nudged off course 90% of the time when flying from the main land to Hawaii.

He also knows that keeping his eye on the destination and making any minor adjustments that are necessary will keep him on course. The same is true with your life. If something isn't working, try something else until you are successful. This will keep you on course. Just keep your eyes on your goals.

Larry Heagney is my Uncle and highly successful in the business world. He was also a D student. He just squeaked through college and law school, but ended up being a highly successful corporate officer at Milliken Textiles and was rewarded well for his efforts. He has now retired from the corporate world and is an extremely successful investor living in an exclusive gated community in Florida. Uncle Larry would always tell me that if I would just be the best at what I was doing, I would always be successful in life. It doesn't matter if you are a doctor, lawyer or garbage man he would say, just be the best and the world will notice. Uncle Larry didn't succeed in the business world because of his education, he succeeded despite his education. If the business world judged him based on his grades, he would have landed a job in the stock room instead of the board room. He would have been given a mop to clean the executive rest rooms, instead of being given the key to it. I know many people that had all the tools and many advantages that my uncle never had, yet never came close to being as successful as Uncle Larry. It isn't what you have that makes you successful; *it is what you do with what you have that makes the difference.*

Abraham Lincoln, being a man of action, said, *"Things may come to those who wait, but only the things left behind by those who hustle"*. It is amazing how many people get bogged down in analyzing, planning, organizing and getting–ready-to-get-ready when what they really need to do is take action and hustle. Just do something! Be aware of your results and if you are not getting the results you want, adjust what you are doing until you get the desired outcome.

A journey of a thousand miles begins with a single step.

—CONFUCIUS

Remember, your journey in life doesn't begin until you take the first step. Take that single step every day and watch your dreams come true. If you want massive results, take massive action on a daily basis, starting today!

Action Steps

Remember, the world doesn't reward us for what we know;
it rewards us for what we do!

This is all you have to do:

1. Write out your goals.

2. Write down the actions you need to take to reach your goals.

3. Schedule at least one action every day toward the fulfillment of those goals, even if it is something small, like planning your meals.

4. Pay attention to the results you are getting and make minor adjustments as necessary.

5. Find people to model and schedule a time to interview them.

6. Develop habits that support you.

7. Take action today. Remember what Thomas Huxley said, "The great end of life is not knowledge, but action."

CHAPTER

$$\boxed{6}$$

Climb Your Ladder of Success with Nutrition

Nothing in the world can take the place of persistence. Talent will not; nothing is more common than unsuccessful men with talent. Genius will not; unrewarded genius is almost a proverb. Education will not; the world is full of educated derelicts.

—CALVIN COOLIDGE

30TH PRESIDENT OF US (1872 - 1933)

This is great news and an extremely important insight! A brilliant life doesn't require an advanced academic degree or a new set of tapes off of a late night infomercial (even if they are only 4 easy payments of $19.95). In fact, you are the most important aspect of your success and the only prerequisite is that you must commit to changing you.

Energy is the fuel to ignite passion and passion is the engine of success. Read that again until it sinks in. Society tells us that we need some elusive ingredient to be successful, but really all you need is the incredible, passionate you. If you desire a passionate life, then you better keep your energy in tact. Your energy flows from three areas. You have a physical, a mental and a spiritual dimension to your energy. If one area is affected, your flow of energy will be hindered. For example, your mind and spirit may be excited about an upcoming project but your body is the vehicle you use to complete the project. If your vehicle is not working properly, you will be stopped dead in your tracks. Fuel your vehicle, however, and you will live the life of your dreams!

This section will show you how to strengthen your body through nutrition, so it will support your mind and spirit for lifelong success. Taking care of your body has four legs just like a table. The legs of your fitness table are Nutrition, Resistance Training, Aerobic Training and Rest & Recovery. Neglect one leg and your fitness table will become unstable. Nurture them all and you will soar! Now let's get to it!

THE FIRST LEG: NUTRITION

Are Diets Really Working?

The second day of a diet is always easier than the first. By the second day you're off it.
—JACKIE GLEASON

If you are looking for a new diet, then you are looking in the wrong place. Don't even consider going any further in this book because this is not a "diet book". This is a book on lifestyle. Yes, I do suggest lifestyle changes with regards to eating but it isn't some new fangled diet. It is the way we were meant to eat all along. In fact, for the most part, it is the way we were told to eat much of our lives by our parents and grandparents. As long as we are on the subject of diets, I think that I should tell you that I believe all fad diets are potentially dangerous and ridiculous. They are ridiculous because they fool you into thinking that you can trick your body. Metabolic tricks are short term and the only one truly tricked is the person doing the tricking. You cannot win a fight against food, so why even try? God gave you food so you can enjoy it, not to torture you with it. It is all about the correct balance.

Unfortunately, the whole fad diet industry is based on the premise of tricking your body and the ever expanding fad diet craze keeps growing, along with the waist line of Americans. Americans are gaining weight and losing money with every new fad diet that comes along. Today we have more fad diets than ever before and Americans are fatter than ever. If fad diets worked, we would not have an obesity epidemic on our hands. Shouldn't that tell you something? You don't need another diet! You just need to learn how to eat so you are satisfied and energized. You don't need to starve yourself. You have to make sure you are eating foods that work with you not against you.

When Napoleon Hill interviewed the wealthiest people of his day, at the request of Andrew Carnegie, health was always at the top of the list of what these great industrialists needed in order to feel successful. Money was towards the bottom. I think they knew that living a vibrant, goal directed life would bring them the financial rewards they were after. After all, if you have all the money in the world, but lose your health, what good does it do?

Recently Ross Patterson, a well known Christian worker contacted me regarding his fitness goals. He knew if he were to stay spiritually strong and vibrant, his body must be strong and vibrant. He didn't want to have just a willing spirit, but he also wanted enough energy for the follow through. While speaking he gave me this quote he had heard, *"When you pray, do not keep on babbling" Matthew 6:7 NIV. Another kind of "babbling" is heard at the dinner table. We sit down to a nutritional nightmare. The grease is bubbling, the salt is glistening, the food is piled up like a mountain, and the sugared drink stands ready to slosh it all down. Then we say "Bless this food to the strength and nourishment of our body." Are you kidding? We are to "honor God with our body" (See 1 Cor. 6:20). Asking God to bless junk food and give it nutritional value is like asking Him to make Detroit the capitol of California."* I'd not heard this one before, but find it totally appropriate.

Let's stop kidding ourselves. Our energy levels and the mirror don't lie. If you aren't eating well, you know it and now you will know what to do about it! After all, isn't that why you are reading this book? Eating is one of the simple pleasures in life. It is also something that you need for energy and growth. If you are eating the correct things at the right time, then you will be more energized, healthy and lean. If you eat the wrong things then you will get tired, fat, weak and sick. By learning how to eat, I will show you how to increase your energy, shed unwanted fat, add muscle and improve your health, all while eating a lot of food. Hear me on this, all while eating a lot of food, not while starving.

Sylvester Stallone says in his book, <u>Sly Moves</u>, *"I gave up dieting years ago and I've never been more in control of my weight. Kicking the diet habit may be the smartest thing you can do to keep your body feeling great."* Not dieting sure seems to have worked for Sly. He is in his 60's and looks spectacular and is more active and vibrant than most people 30 years his junior. I know it will work for you, too. As a side note, a few years ago we saw Sly on TV and I asked my wife how I looked compared to him. I said, "I know I am quite a bit younger but what do you think?" She said that his shoulders were better than mine and boy did that spur me on. That wasn't exactly the answer I was looking for and I found myself wishing for a wife who lied a little bit more, but it did motivate me. I have been doing some carefully controlled shoulder exercises and think my shoulders are better than Sly's now. How about it Sly, lets do a "Shoulder Show Down" on Oprah or Larry King. Oh man, I need to start training hard now in case he takes me up on it, because he looks incredible regardless of his age. Oh…maybe I should have addressed you as Mr. Stallone…Sir.

Eat CLEAN to be LEAN!

Whether you want to look like Sylvester Stallone, or just want to be the best "you" you can be, you must have a lifestyle that incorporates eating properly in order to stay fit and energetic. Overwhelming studies have shown that when people diet; they inevitably come off the diet and gain even more weight. You will see the phrase, *"eating clean,"* a lot in this book. That is the phrase that bodybuilders, world class athletes, models and celebrities use. I think it is a very descriptive word for the way we should eat. It basically means eating foods that work with your metabolism, not against it. Foods that will make you more energetic feel better and look better. They are foods that are natural, like lean proteins, fresh raw or slightly cooked vegetables, whole grains and fruits. Basically avoid "unclean foods" which are concentrated in calories and will make us fat and weak. An example of a concentrated calorie is any food that contains a lot of calories, but takes up little room in your stomach. By eating only whole, natural, unprocessed foods, you will avoid most concentrated calorie foods. I don't know anyone that has gotten fat or overeaten on apples and broccoli, but we have all gotten carried away with pizza, cookies, cake and ice-cream. Haven't we?

METABOLIC MISFORTUNE

People are always looking for a free ride. That is why all of these fad diets are so appealing. There is NO miraculous way to fat loss other than good nutritional and exercise practices. With all the thousands of foods to choose from you can see how "diet gurus" can come up with different miracle foods and combinations of foods for the next diet frenzy. It is endless. The bottom line is, when you go on some of these diets you can damage your metabolism.

The typical weight loss from fad diets is water weight, then fat and muscle mass. The loss of muscle mass is where the metabolic misfortune begins because this inhibits the body's natural ability to burn calories. Muscle burns more calories than fat, even at rest. So when the dieter has lost muscle weight, they have also lost the ability to burn calories because they have less muscle. The dieter is injuring his or her own metabolism instead of working with their metabolism by eating properly. To make matters worse, most dieters eventually return to their old pattern of eating and tend to gain all the weight they lost and then some more because they have less muscle available to burn calories. They then go on another diet, lose more muscle and then have an even higher percentage of body fat and the cycle continues until the person finally gives up, being much fatter then when they started. This is an incredibly sad and needless cycle, there is a better way. It is simply called eating right, just like you are learning in this book.

When I was a kid my mother had a real struggle with her weight. She tried every diet, had some success, and then gained all the weight back and more. My dad always told her that the best exercise she could do to lose weight was to push herself away from the dinner table. In other words, eat less. Many years later, both of my parents look great. My mother hasn't dieted in years and she has kept the weight off for decades by eating properly and doing moderate exercise.

I have never known anyone to stick to a diet forever. I have, however, known people that have changed their lifestyle and have taken control of their bodies and their lives. These people that started eating whole foods were satisfied so that they felt good when they walked away from the dinner table. So let's learn how to eat properly and enjoy eating.

EAT THE WEIGHT OFF!

The more active you are, the more you have to eat in order to keep your energy levels high. Don't have an attitude of lack. I don't know about you, but I don't want to be limited. I want abundance in my life and I want to be satisfied when I eat, so I eat a lot and I eat often. Take my lead and eat foods that will work with your body and metabolism to make you stronger, healthier, fitter, leaner and more energetic. In fact, did you know that <u>eating increases your metabolism</u>? It doesn't slow it down. *If you are overweight, eat the weight off, don't starve it off.* <u>Just eat "clean"</u>.

The more often you eat, the more your body gets used to processing food so you lose fat and increase your energy, because your body uses this food for energy. When you don't eat regularly and often, your body goes into starvation mode. It is a protection mechanism that allows your body to store calories as fat, so they can be used later. Is it any wonder why most people who diet get fatter, flabbier and more discontent with dieting? Isn't it incredible that with all of the diets of the day, that we have a fatter society? You don't need to diet. You need to make some simple lifestyle changes and eat only good, clean, natural and unprocessed foods.

You don't have to be confused by the ever-changing advice about what to eat and what to avoid. This hasn't changed in thousands of years, so we are not in danger of it changing now. Don't worry if you don't know the latest version of the food pyramid by heart! Experts from the Mayo Clinic say eating right really boils down to a few basics:

- Consume more fruits, vegetables, and whole grains.
- Cut cholesterol and saturated fats.
- Limit sweets and salt.
- Drink alcohol in moderation, if at all.
- Monitor your daily calorie intake.
- Eat moderate portion sizes.

So now that we have this clear, you can just eat right! Of course don't forget to get plenty of low fat proteins like protein powders, chicken breast, turkey breast, fish, egg whites, lean meats, etc. And don't forget PLENTY OF WATER.

A good buddy of mine, Mitch Mayer, lives in Southampton, New York. We have been close friends for nearly 20 years and in all the time I have known him, he has stayed one of the fittest people I know. I also might mention that he eats more than a small country. But I have to tell you that he can eat so much because he eats "clean". Mitch is 10 years older than me, and looks just like he did 20 years ago with the exception of a few distinguished gray hairs. I say a "few" because he only has a few hairs left.

At 57 years old, Mitch is first and foremost a dedicated husband and father. He is also a busy real estate investor and broker, as well as an active member of his community and he travels. I'd also like to share with you that year after year; Mitch is the friend I'd mentioned before who passes with flying colors the rigorous life guarding tests and earns a position as a lifeguard every summer at a Montauk Point beach, beating out many half his age and more. He has more energy than most 20 year olds and is showing no signs of slowing down. He doesn't have to put a ton of time and energy into being healthy and energetic because his "lifestyle" has always been a lifestyle that promotes health and energy.

If you ask Mitch, he will tell you to eat a lot but "eat clean". He eats plenty of lean protein, fresh fruits & vegetables, whole grains and mostly foods produced by nature. Once, I accidentally tried putting half and half in his coffee at Starbucks and I thought he would have a stroke. *"What are you trying to do? KILL ME!?!?"* he shouted. (He only uses skim milk). Now when I want to give him a hard time, I make believe I am putting half and half in his coffee. But he is on to me and I don't get that fun response very often. Mitch is dedicated to eating properly, so he can continue to "show up" the young life guards every summer and keep up with his energetic wife, Alexis, and son, Morgan, which is no easy task.

People are begging for solutions and are willing to pay big bucks for them. That is why there is a new diet every time we turn around. Diet marketers try to come up with a new concept or a fancy name. They spend a ton of time and money marketing it to a bunch of desperate consumers. You don't HAVE to spend a ton of money on pre-measured food plans. There are principles that govern your body. These principles have been in existence since the beginning of time. This is not something new, not something that you weren't aware of. I am just putting it all together in one place so you can reference it and get into the best shape of your life. I am boiling it all down to only the things that work and can be implemented into your daily life. Regardless of whether you are a professional athlete, pastor, household executive, corporate executive, construction worker, missionary, business owner, grandparent or a weekend warrior, abide by these principles and you will flourish. Break them and as you know, you will pay the price.

Genetics vs. Conditioning

I know so many people that say "I don't have any chance at all, my mom or my dad was _____(insert word here), so I have no a chance at living a healthy, vibrant life." The question I always have is "why"? I know genetics plays a role, but so does our conditioning. Most of the people that I know who are tired and over weight and say they have a "genetic" disposition for it, eat exactly like their parents did or have conditioned themselves to eat poorly. Again, is it genetics or conditioning? I have no scientific study to back this up, only my own observations and I vote for conditioning, 99% of the time.

I know many families where the majority of the people in that family are either very over weight or obese and then a few within the same family who aren't. Many times the people burden themselves with the genetic thing by believing that they may be pre-disposed. Keep in mind many forms of diabetes and cancer are tied to obesity and/or poor lifestyle choices. Again, is this genetics or is it the conditioning that the parents did with their children, or simply bad habits these people have developed over the years? In these same families, I know some of the adult children that get regular exercise and eat a clean diet and aren't obese, in fact they are in exceptionally good shape. Genetics or conditioning...well you already know my answer. My thought is, let's not use genetics as a crutch and let's try to do our best with what we have. Be responsible and inform your physician of genetic predispositions but let's do our best to overcome some of the problems our ancestors may have had by eating properly and exercising daily.

I once heard about these twin boys that were interviewed as adults. One was highly successful, the other one an alcoholic. Their father was an alcoholic. When interviewed the highly successful son was asked," How come you are so successful and aren't an alcoholic?" He said, "I had no choice, you see my dad was an alcoholic and I didn't want to end up like him." The alcoholic brother was asked the same question and his answer was astonishing. He said almost the same thing with a twist. "He said he had no choice...because his father was an alcoholic." The choice is yours. If you had some bad examples while growing up, you can break them in your life by deciding to change. The choice is yours.

The bottom line is this, if you are eating only natural, whole, unprocessed foods that energize you and make you healthy, then you are putting the odds in your favor with regards to your overall health.

Action Steps

*Remember, the world doesn't reward us for what we know;
it rewards us for what we do!*

1. Don't diet.
2. "Eat clean"
3. Eat often--at least five to six times per day.

4. Eat the weight off.

5. Read labels, avoid high-fructose corn syrup and other known killers.

6. Stock up on natural, unprocessed whole foods like lean protein, whole grains, fruits and vegetables.

CHAPTER

$$\boxed{7}$$

Fuel Your Body for Spectacular Health and Energy

WHAT TO EAT WHILE CLIMBING THE LADDER OF SUCCESS

Eat a well balanced diet *"almost"* like grandma used to make. Grandma always told you to eat your meat and veggies, and she was right. We are just going to leave out the mashed potatoes, stuffing and desserts. I have learned from elite athletes who consistently maintain low body fat and lean hard muscle, that you can keep your calories relatively high and still burn body fat simply by eating more protein in place of carbohydrates at your meals. You should be eating less, but not zero carbohydrates and eating more fiber, which you will get in the unprocessed natural foods you will be eating. Fiber improves digestion, burns fat and keeps your blood sugar levels stable, giving you steady energy throughout the day.

What we are talking about is an eating plan, not a diet. I can't stress that enough. You will be eating probably more than you eat now, just different stuff. You will be eating at least five to six times a day and maybe more. Now before you freak out, let me tell you that I count the snack time as a meal. We are going to make the snacks COUNT! You will be eating lean protein, fruits, vegetables and whole grains. You will also drink a lot of water. Since your blood sugar levels will be level all the time, you will notice that you have plenty of energy and vigor. Those are two of the ingredients to living a passionate life. It is hard to have passion and enthusiasm when you have no "oomph".

PROTEIN

Protein is the name of the game, Baby! I am not going to get into a scientific explanation of protein and amino acids. I want to keep this simple. I just want you to model what successfully fit people do. Do what they do and you will have what they have!

If you are looking to stay or get lean, energetic, strong and healthful, you must eat protein. What you eat is just as important as what you don't eat. Proteins are the building blocks of your body. Protein allows your body to heal itself and protein is also what makes your muscles grow and they are what keep you lean. Remember muscle burns more calories than fat, even at rest. You need lots of protein to build and maintain muscle. Just be sure that you are eating protein that is low in fat. The list below will help you out.

Quality sources of protein

- Chicken breast
- Turkey breast
- Extra lean ground turkey breast or chicken
- Extra lean ground beef
- Buffalo/bison
- Lean game meats like venison
- Fish (broiled, baked, grilled, not fried)
- Egg whites
- Nonfat or low fat cottage cheese
- Top round steak (the leanest cut of red meat)
- Protein powder supplements (whey, casein, or a combination) (Be sure to check the sodium, calorie and cholesterol content in these. Some are very high. The lower the numbers the better.)

How much protein?

The rule of thumb is at least 1 gram of protein per pound of body weight. For example, a 200 pound person would take at least 200 grams of protein. This is a unisex rule. It doesn't matter if you are a man or a woman. It is still 1 gram of protein per pound of body weight. It is that simple. Don't worry. I will give you an easy way to measure your protein out in a minute.

If you are trying to add muscle and lose fat, you need more protein. Let me explain. One gram of protein per pound of body weight is the bare minimum. I suggest that most people start off with this amount for the first month or two and then increase it from there. If, however, you are trying to put on muscle or burn fat, you may need up to 1.25 to 1.5 grams. Once you are doing this for a while, you'll know how much you need and can adjust up or down to meet your particular needs.

Okay now, how do you measure your protein? It is very easy. 20 grams of protein is a serving. A 20 gram serving is approximately the size of a deck of cards. Unless you are a competitive bodybuilder or model, this is close enough. Also, most of the time, one scoop of protein powder will be approximately 20 grams of protein, but read the label. You can get that information from the protein container.

So let's go back to our examples. A 200 pound man would need at least 10 portions of protein during the day. 200 pounds = 200 grams of protein, divided by 20 grams of protein = 10 portions.

Below is a simple chart that will help you. You don't need to go crazy counting your protein intake, just use this as a guide and do the best you can. I am going to make this very easy for you, so you can focus on your passions in life.

Body Weight	# OF SERVINGS FOR 1 GRAM/LB	# OF SERVINGS FOR 1.25 GRAMS/LB	# OF SERVINGS FOR 1.5 GRAMS/LB
100	5	6	8
110	6	7	8
120	6	8	9
130	7	8	10
140	7	9	11
150	8	9	11

160	8	10	12
170	9	11	13
180	9	11	14
190	10	12	14
200	10	13	15
210	11	13	16
220	11	14	17
230	12	14	17
240	12	15	18
250	13	16	19
260	13	16	20
270	14	17	20
280	14	18	21
290	15	18	22
300	15	19	23
310	16	19	23
320	16	20	24
330	17	21	25
340	17	21	26
350	18	22	26

The above portions are based on bodyweight. For many years, I told people to throw their scales away because body weight is not an accurate portrayal of your fitness level. Since muscle is heavier than fat, you could be getting in better shape, but be heavier. Now, I tell them to get out their scales. A scale is necessary to help figure out your protein requirements and to help in the measuring of progress. Now, you can also buy scales that measure your body fat. I have one that costs around $100.00 and recently, when I had my body fat tested at the gym on their elaborate computer based system, it came back as the same body fat and weight my home scale gives me. This may be something you want to consider as you progress in your fitness regimen, so you can monitor your results more effectively. I find using the body fat scale fun. It is interesting to monitor my results and to make sure that I am going in the right direction as far as my body fat goes. You may also like to do this.

FIBER

Protein will definitely put you in the fat burning zone, but fiber will keep you there. When fiber is digested, it ferments in the gut and gets converted into short chain fatty acids, which can be used by the body for fuel. This process, in turn, sends a signal to the fat cells to release fat and to use it for energy.

In other words, just eat your fiber and you will look and feel better.

We need to consume at least 25 to 30 grams of fiber a day. This seems like a lot of fiber, especially compared to how we eat today. The average person is lucky if he gets 12 grams of fiber per day. According to the American Heart Association (AHA), fiber is important for lowering cholesterol and body fat, as well as for the health of our digestive system. Both the AHA and the National Cancer Institute recommend that we consume 25 to 30 grams of fiber a day. I personally try to get 50 grams a day and when I do, I feel great. An easy way to consume this much fiber is by using a high fiber cereal. I personally like to eat whole grains like oat groats, kamut, rye, etc., that I buy in bulk at my local health food store. I will usually cook up the grains, add 2 scoops (40 grams) of whey protein powder and add chopped apple, pear and/or raisins into it for breakfast, (and because I like the taste I like to add almond extract or ground cinnamon which is also good for you) This gives me plenty of fiber, good protein, good carbohydrates and leaves me satisfied for a long time. Can't get the time to make your cereal the old fashioned way? There are many cereals on the market today that are high in fiber and delicious too like Fiber One.

If you eat a high fiber cereal and your fruits and vegetables during the day with your protein, you will be getting plenty of fiber. I also supplement my protein shakes with phylum husk. I get the kind that has no sugar. You can get this in any food or drug store. I just add a tablespoon to every shake that I have. A tablespoon with a large glass of water works well, too. You don't have to be crazy with recording all your fiber, just make sure you are getting close to the right amount. By following some of my tricks, you should have no problem getting the fiber that you need.

The Mayo Clinic gives these tips for fitting more fiber into your diet:

Start your day with a high-fiber breakfast cereal — 5 or more grams of fiber per serving. Opt for cereals with "bran" or "fiber" in the name. Read the labels. You will be able to check the fiber grams per serving there. I suggest that you add a few tablespoons of unprocessed wheat bran to your favorite cereal.

- Add crushed bran cereal or unprocessed wheat bran to baked products such as meatloaf, breads, muffins, casseroles, cakes and cookies. You can also use bran products as a crunchy topping for casseroles, salads or cooked vegetables.

- Switch to whole-grain breads. These breads list whole wheat, whole-wheat flour or another whole grain as the first ingredient on the label. Look for a brand with at least 2 grams of dietary fiber per serving. *Note: We are also cautious to avoid buying breads with high fructose corn syrup.*

- Substitute whole-grain flour for half or all of the white flour when baking bread. Whole-grain flour is heavier than white flour. In yeast breads, use a bit more yeast or let the dough rise longer. When using baking powder, increase it by 1 teaspoon for every 3 cups of whole-grain flour.

- Eat more whole grains and whole-grain products. Experiment with brown rice, barley, whole-wheat pasta and bulgur.

- Take advantage of ready-to-use vegetables. Mix chopped frozen broccoli into prepared spaghetti sauce. Snack on baby carrots.

- Eat more beans, peas and lentils. Add kidney beans to canned soup or a green salad. Or make nachos with refried black beans, baked tortilla chips and fresh salsa.

- Eat fruit at every meal. Apples, berries, oranges, pears and bananas, are good sources of fiber.

- Make snacks count. Fresh fruit, raw vegetables, low-fat popcorn and whole-grain crackers are all good choices.

High-fiber foods are good for your health and they fill you up, so it makes eating more satisfying. But adding too much fiber too quickly can cause intestinal gas, abdominal bloating and cramping *(If you find that people are staying away from you, you may have increased your fiber too fast)*. Increase fiber in your diet gradually over a period of a few weeks. This allows the natural bacteria in your digestive system to adjust to the change. Also, drink plenty of water. Fiber works best when it absorbs water, making your stool soft and bulky. Without the added water, you could become constipated.

Dennis Lairon, a researcher at the French National Health institute, told Reuters Health that, *"adults would do well to get more than the recommended fiber intake of roughly 25 grams per day."* He also added that, *"for each 5 gram increase above that was linked to a greater decrease in the risks of being overweight or having high blood pressure or high cholesterol. People can generally have fiber intakes of up to 70 grams a day without having digestive symptoms such as bloating and cramping"*, Lairon told Reuters Health.

The Top Five Fiber Foods

This list can serve as a general guide.

1. Bran cereals
2. Fruits. Raspberries and Blueberries are some of the highest in fiber.
3. Vegetables.
4. Whole grains.
5. Nuts. Especially almonds. (Consume these sparingly, because of their high fat content.).

CARBOHYDRATES

The Good, the Bad and the Ugly of Carbohydrates

Carbohydrates are not the evil demons of the food world. There are good carbs and bad carbs. Today, it is very vogue to despise ALL carbs and make them the fall guy in our quest for health and fitness. Many diets promote a high protein diet with little or no carbs. This gets back to trying to trick your metabolism. It will not work...for very long! Plus, it is a horrible and very un-satisfying way to eat.

Those who stick to the high-fat, high-protein, and low or no-carbohydrate diets may risk long-term health problems. High protein diets that eliminate carbs, trigger short-term weight loss through a process called ketosis. Ketosis occurs whenever the body lacks a sufficient supply of carbohydrates, a prime source of energy. During ketosis, carbohydrate-depleted metabolisms turn to other sources, including ketones from stored fat or protein, to satisfy daily energy needs. (This is the very situation that diabetics try to avoid.) You will lose weight. Most of the weight loss is water weight, followed by the carbohydrates that are in your muscles, and then as you progress on this diet you will lose some fat.....but you will also lose muscle mass. You lose muscle which means you have less muscle to burn fat. Hence, you are on the diet roller coaster with no end in sight. Some people can do this for a short time to jump start their weight loss program, but most people will overeat once they stop this diet and are in worse shape then when they started.

This type of diet can have a negative long-term impact on your health. It's high in cholesterol and total fat -- the opposite of what all the health organizations, from the American Heart Association to the American Dietetic Association, recommend. The diet is also low in fruits, vegetables and whole grains -- foods that have proven health benefits and leave you full and satisfied after a meal. You end up losing out on the vitamins and minerals that are in these foods not to mention other benefits -- like fiber. Sounds silly doesn't it?

The Good

You'll find good carbs in your fruit, vegetable and whole grain sections of your grocery or health food store. Fresh fruit, raw or slightly cooked vegetables and whole grains will leave you satisfied for hours and it's almost impossible to overeat them. You will know that you ate good carbs, when you have energy all day. You can recognize bad carbs, because you are ready for a nap after eating them.

The Bad

We don't need much reminding of what bad carbs are. They are the highly processed ones that are low in fiber and deliver a quick jolt to your blood sugar levels. Once your blood sugar levels plummet, usually an hour or so later, you start craving more and more carbohydrates. It's that never ending cycle that causes people to overeat.

Oh yeah. Bad carbs are easy to pick out in a line up. They are the delicious, mouth watering ones. The ones you dream about. The ones you bring to Grandma's house to show her that you love her. Wait a minute. I am getting carried away. They are bad! Yes, very bad...but we all love them. I'd better hurry through this chapter before I start raiding my kid's snacks. They are made out of white flour, white sugar, etc. They are the ones that I want late at night, when I can't sleep. Once I eat some, I sleep like a baby. Bad carbs are usually made with white: white bread, white rice, white potatoes, any dessert made with white flour and many of the starchy carbs. I know many people that have just cut white carbs out of their diets and lost a ton of weight. I read something on Oprah Winfrey and she says she can't eat white bread, rice, flour etc., but she can eat whole wheat pasta and breads in moderation. Simply stay away from highly processed foods. Get it as close to the way it was grown as possible and you will be fine.

The Ugly

Rutabagas. Yes they are an ugly carbohydrate to look at, but then again beauty is in the eye of the beholder. I had to put something under this heading because I liked the main heading "the good, the bad and the ugly of carbohydrates." I don't know much about the rutabaga and in an effort to avoid hate mail from the rutabaga lovers, I just want you to know that this is a joke to end this section, not a review on rutabagas. Now that this is settled we can get into fats.

FATS

Are you getting enough fat?

The trend over the last 20 years was to take fat out of everything, so we would be healthier. Oh! Did I say that out loud? Did I blow the big fat, FAT conspiracy? Well, what has happened over the past 20 years is that as we took fat out of our diets and we got fatter. It just goes to show you that God gave us protein, carbohydrates, fats and water for a reason. I guess He knew what He was doing. Don't get me wrong. Eating a low fat diet is essential. I am not saying you should start eating high fat butter, start chomping on high fat bacon with your whole eggs and washing it down with a gallon of whole milk. What I am saying is that you should have some fat, the right fat, in your diet for health reasons.

We need fat in our diet for many reasons. Fat protects our organs. It protects and repairs the walls of our cells, regulates our body temperature, keeps skin and hair healthy, and leaves us feeling fuller after a meal, so we won't go and eat a gallon of fat free ice cream for dessert. Vitamins like A, D, E and K cannot be absorbed by the body without the right fat in our diet. I eat a pretty low fat diet, but I add fats like olive oil and fish oils to my diet to fulfill my need for fat.

The Skinny on Fats. Good Fat VS. Bad Fat.

We all are aware that high-fat diets have been linked to an increased risk of heart disease, certain types of cancer and obesity. Most major health organizations recommend limiting total fat intake for many health-related issues. Not only is the amount of fat important in reducing health risks, but the type of fat is also important. Understanding the differences between the three types of fat (saturated, monounsaturated and polyunsaturated) will allow you to make intelligent eating choices.

Saturated fats are usually solid at room temperature and are largely found in meats and dairy foods such as whole milk, cream, regular ice cream, cheese and butter. Some vegetable fats are very high in saturated fat like palm, palm kernel, and coconut oils. Eating foods high in saturated fat can wreak havoc on your blood cholesterol levels and increase your health risks. In fact, saturated fat increases your blood cholesterol level, especially the bad LDL cholesterol, more than anything else you eat. This is an easy one. Stay away from them!

Transfats act like saturated fat and raise LDL cholesterol. They may also lower the good HDL cholesterol. Stay away from everything made with hydrogenated or partially hydrogenated shortening.

When substituted for saturated fat in the diet, monounsaturated fat may lower harmful LDL cholesterol leaving the beneficial HDL cholesterol unchanged. Olive oil, canola oil and most nuts are high in monounsaturated fat. Even though these are good, you still want to use them in moderation. I personally use extra virgin olive oil with each meal and even add it to my protein drinks to leave me satisfied for a longer period of time. I have different olive oils in my home and they taste great, especially some of the finer oils! They are made with the same care as a fine wine. Unlike a fine wine, the fresher the olive oil the better. I like the ones from the Mediterranean regions, particularly Italy, Spain and Greece. Keep in mind that the people in the Mediterranean regions have a very low occurrence of coronary artery disease.

Polyunsaturated fat may also help lower blood cholesterol levels when substituted for saturated fat. Foods rich in polyunsaturated fat include vegetable oils like corn, safflower, soybean, and sunflower seed oil, as well as margarine, and most salad dressings. One downside to this type of fat is that while it lowers the bad LDL cholesterol, it may also lower the good HDL cholesterol. Moderation is the key with these also. I personally severely limit these types of fats and try to get most of my fats from olive oil and fish oils.

Omega-3 fatty acids may help decrease heart disease by lowering triglyceride levels, increasing HDL levels and decreasing blood clotting and inflammation. Omega-3 fatty acid is found in fish. Other sources include flaxseed, soybeans and walnuts. You can also get an omega-3 fatty acid supplement. This is what I do as a precaution. I take a liquid fish oil. Eating fish is a great way to increase your omega-3 fatty acids. Be careful with the nuts. Eat them in moderation.

The most important thing to remember is that eating too much fat of any kind increases your risk for obesity. Use even your good fats in moderation and choose monounsaturated and polyunsaturated fats over saturated fat.

Water

Have you heard about the "magic" pill that makes you slimmer and that also increases energy and generates firmer skin? Wouldn't it be great if it really worked? Turns out that the magic's not in the pill but in the water you wash it down with. How important is water to our bodies? Consider that your body can survive approximately 40 days without food, but only 7 days without water. Amazingly, the body can lose up to 50% of it's protein, while a loss of even 10% of it's water causes severe physical problems. A 20% loss of water may even cause death.

Water helps rid the body of fat by metabolizing stored fat into energy. The body also uses water to rid itself of toxins, aids in circulation and joint lubrication and increases energy. Water helps regulate your body temperature. It is important for transferring oxygen throughout you body. It helps in the distribution vitamins, minerals and other nutrients throughout your body. Water may be the only true "magic pill" for permanent weight loss, better health and vibrant energy. Water curbs the appetite and I find when I am drinking enough water, I have fewer cravings for sweets.

So ask yourself: Are you getting enough water?

You've probably heard it somewhere before that a person should drink eight 8-ounce glasses of water every day. As it turns out, that's just the beginning. Since every human being is designed differently, a more suitable solution is to drink half your body weight in ounces. It might sound like a lot, but considering that your brain tissue is made up of 85 percent water, it's crucial that you're giving your body what it needs to live a vibrant life. I personally try to drink a gallon of water a day. Some days I make it. Most days I fall short. You need to find the right amount that works for you and drink it every day.

Water is the most over-looked resource for our bodies. Inexpensive and in most cases free, yet we shun it like an inconvenience and a waste of our precious time. Water is a natural resource that helps you with weight loss, health, muscle gain, longevity, and other positive things that we want for our bodies. Yet, we don't drink enough.. "Since it is free, how good could it be for you?" is the thought. If you don't like the taste, do what I do and add lemon juice, which is a simple solution. Also drinking it cool, instead of ice cold, makes it easier to drink more water. Drink water and drink it often.

Action Steps

Remember, the world doesn't reward us for what we know;
it rewards us for what we do!

1. Make a shopping list for your protein to make sure you have plenty.
2. Start tracking your protein intake to make sure you are getting enough.
3. Keep an eye on your fiber to make sure you are getting enough.
4. Make sure you are eating the right carbohydrates
5. Make sure you are getting the right fats.
6. Make sure you are getting enough water

This is pretty simple. Just eat lean low fat protein, good unprocessed carbohydrates, good fats and water. Keep an eye on this and you can eat a lot and often. All while getting into the best shape of your life and becoming more vibrant!

CHAPTER

$$\boxed{8}$$

Climb Your Ladder of Success Eating Plan

HOW TO EAT

I know there are so many books out there that tell you what to do, but not how to do it. I want to make this as easy as possible for you to be successful. This is a real basic eating plan. Simply eat five or six meals a day or more, dividing your protein, fats, carbs, etc. among those meals. These meals will probably be a bit smaller than the serving sizes you are used to now, but don't worry, you are eating more often. You'll need to stay within the general daily range of total calorie intake, but you don't have to go crazy counting calories. I could never count calories and I don't know many that can. Some engineer types may thrive on counting calories, but being exact isn't necessary. If that is something that flips your switch, then go for it. For the rest of us, just eat clean and often.

My eating style and philosophy

My eating style is moderate in natural carbohydrates, low in fat but not too low, with plenty of good quality protein. Sounds simple, doesn't it?. Being fit and energetic isn't complicated; people just try to make it sound that way. I personally don't count calories at all or figure out percentages of food. I simply have six to eight meals a day. (Protein drinks count as a meal) I eat lean protein, fresh fruits and vegetables and whole grains, plus plenty of water. That is it in a nut shell. This is very simple, very delicious and very satisfying.

Make eating bad inconvenient

If unhealthy foods are easy to get to you will eat them, unless you are made of stone. If they are sitting on a shelf or in the refrigerator right in front of you, they will taunt you. I don't know about you, but I can handle just about anything but the seduction of food.

Make unhealthy, energy depleting, fattening foods hard to get to. If you have older kids, this gets a little more difficult, but not impossible. Little kids will only be able to eat what you bring into the house, but the older kids will sometimes go out and buy their own stuff and bring it home. Since my children are mostly grown, they now bring their own snacks into the house. If my kids want to get something that will tempt me, they have two choices, eat it right away or hide it. If it is something that will call my name and taunt me, I throw it away. Since Dad may throw their stuff away, it causes them to think twice about getting these types of foods for themselves. When they were young, we didn't bring this stuff into the house except for the occasional treat. Childhood obesity is a national nightmare and getting worse, so I don't feel bad about making eating poorly difficult for my children. In fact, I feel it is my responsibility as a parent.

Sometimes, if all else fails, you just have to resort to good, old fashioned, self-control. Most people are conditioned to eat everything that is put in front of them, which could be a recipe for disaster. When you are out, you need to pick and choose what you will eat. Eating on a regular basis and keeping your blood sugar levels steady, will make self-control much easier. Make a list and buy what's ON the list. Most people that I know, eat the same things on a regular basis. This will help you to keep things around the house that will empower you to achieve your goals.

Plan your meals for the week, so it is easy. Here are some ideas of what your sample menu may look like. Now keep in mind, most of my meals look the same, especially breakfast and my protein drinks. I just jotted this down so you could get some ideas.

SAMPLE MENUS	
MEAL	MEAL
Steel Cut Irish Oatmeal Egg Whites Almond Extract Olive Oil Splenda Coffee I mix the oatmeal, egg whites, almond extract, Olive Oil & Splenda in a bowl and microwave. I stir it often. It is a delicious breakfast!	Protein shake and fruit Water

Protein shake with added fiber and fruit Water	Grilled chicken Steamed or fresh vegetables Water with lemon
Turkey sandwich on spelt or whole grain bread with olive oil, lettuce and tomato (often I leave out the bread all together and I make sure the turkey is lower in cholesterol and I have lots of it) Water	Protein shake with added olive oil or Protein pudding

SUPPLEMENTS

An entire industry has been borne out of the need to supplement our nutritionally deficient food supply. Although there are many supplements that will benefit your quest for outstanding health and energy, there are also many that do nothing. They just create expensive urine.

I am going to give you what I feel is necessary, but keep in mind that this is a bare bones list. Many people that are involved with sports may need additional supplementation and those that are extremely obese may also need supplemental assistance. I don't want to give that specific nutritional advice in this book because it would be irresponsible. But for the average, healthy person this list should be adequate. Always remember that the best supplement is real, whole food.

What I recommend….. In fact, what I take myself:

- **Whey protein**. I use whey protein as soon as I wake up because it gets digested quickly. After sleeping 8 hours your muscles need quick nourishment. I also use whey protein after my workouts and during the day to help me meet my protein requirements. If I want to feel more satisfied or if I want this protein drink to digest slower, I usually put in a little olive oil and phylum husk. This slows down the digestion, plus gives me the added benefit of my good fat.

- **Meal replacement drinks**. These are usually a mixture of whey and casein protein. Casein is slower to digest and makes you feel full longer. This will really help during the day if you are hungry but don't have time to eat. It is a very convenient way to get your protein. I don't use many of these unless I am traveling but they sure are convenient to have in the refrigerator.

- **Multi-vitamin**. I personally use a multi-vitamin pack that has several pills. Just look around for a good multi-vitamin and/or a multi-vitamin pack.

- **Green tea**. I find that green tea gives me more energy and makes me feel good. It also has anti-oxidants in it, so it is good for you. I like the way it tastes and sweeten it with Splenda. You can also get green tea in pill form. It's worth a try.

- **Glucosamine and chondroitin**. I use these in a single pill that I get at a super store near my home. It is great for your joints and has made my knees feel much better. My knees took a beating during my athletics training and then got banged up really badly in the car accident that ended my running career. In fact, the doctors told me I would have severe arthritis by the time I was 40. Well, I am 47 and feel great. Let's hear it for the fitness lifestyle!!

- **Super greens**. You can get these 'green foods' in your local health food store. They are in powder form and have a lot of detoxifying ingredients, vitamins, minerals, etc. This is an easy way to make sure your body is being fed all of it's nutrients. I always keep a container in my cupboard, but I must admit, I don't take it very often. Hey, just do what I say, not as I do.

- **Protein bars**. This is tricky these days with the many pseudo-protein bars out there. They can be a good source of protein, but make sure that it is not a glorified candy bar. Make sure the sugars are low, no fructose, etc. I rarely eat these and I am extremely picky about the ones I use.

- **Flax seed and/or flax seed oil**. This is good for over-all health and cholesterol levels.

- **Fish oil**. I personally take a liquid fish oil that is delicious and very good for you.

- **Creatine**. I like creatine for when I am training with weights. Do your home work on this and all supplements before taking them.

For all of the above supplements and any others that you may want to try, you will want to find a store that has a knowledgeable staff so they can make sure you are finding the proper products.   It is in your best interest, if you are going to spend money on food supplements that you find out what is good and what isn't. I deliberately did not tell you what brands to use, because things change daily in this business. Look around and speak to knowledgeable people. Use the internet. It is an incredible resource of information for your healthy lifestyle. Do your homework.

Well, that is it for how to eat. You can make it much more complicated. But why would you want to do that? Like I said, taking care of your body has four legs just like a table. We just covered the leg of nutrition. Next we will cover resistance training, then aerobic training, and rest & recovery. This way you will not neglect any of the legs on your fitness table, making it very stable and well balanced so it supports you and your active lifestyle.

Action Steps

Remember, the world doesn't reward us for what we know;
it rewards us for what we do!

1. Don't diet. Eat!
2. Eat 5 to 6 meals a day or more.
3. Eat plenty of lean protein. Try to get a minimum of 1 gram of protein for every pound of body weight.
4. Eat plenty of fresh fruits, vegetables and whole grains.
5. Up your fiber intake. #4 will help with this one.
6. Drink plenty of water.

CHAPTER

$$\boxed{9}$$

The Power of Fitness!

Physical fitness is not only one of the most important keys to a healthy body, it is the basis of dynamic and creative intellectual activity. —**JOHN F. KENNEDY**

Now you know how to eat to super charge your energy and transform your body! Let's take a look at the other three legs of your fitness table: Resistance Training, Aerobic Training (cardiovascular) and Rest & Recovery. By the time you finish, you will have all of the tools you will need to have your body totally support you. Remember, *YOU* are the most important ingredient to *your* success equation. You will have the energy and strength to fuel your passion and, as you know, passion is the engine that will drive your success to incredible new heights.

Successercise

I love the term *Successercise*. No, it is not a real word....yet. But it should be. This book is not just about eating and exercising correctly. It is about having the energy to succeed at all levels. It's about you and having energy to support your lifestyle. You and your body are not two separate things. Both are required, if you are going to climb your ladder of success without running out of gas.

Jim Anthony owns Anthony and Company, a commercial real estate company, in Raleigh, N.C. He knows that energy and passion are the keys to success so he started the "Anthony and Company Stair Challenge". In this challenge, he and his employees mark a sheet of paper every time they climb the stairs from the entrance to the staircase to their fourth floor office suite instead of taking the elevator. Jim knows a healthier body gives you more energy and focus, plus pays big dividends in a competitive workplace. Jim is very fit, strong and energetic and encourages those around him to stay fit. He eats very well, works out regularly and is a big believer in the body, mind and spirit approach to success. Jim also happens to be very competitive and his name is usually number one on the list.

The Second Leg: Resistance Training

Use it or loose it

Right from the beginning, we were designed to work. Work is not a dirty word. It keeps you young. Working your body is important. If you don't use your body you will lose it. Period! No ifs, ands or buts. Come on. You see it every day. People who don't move very much, eventually get to the point where it becomes harder and harder to move at all. Conversely, we all know people who are vibrant and energetic at older ages. My grandmother told me once, *"Your legs carry you into old age, so keep your legs strong."* My grandmother turned 102 years of age in November of 2006. She has kept her legs strong, which in turn carried her into old age with all of her wits. At her 100th birthday party, she knew the name of every grandchild, great-grandchild and great, great-grandchild. And she did all of this with failing vision. She used her hearing to identify everyone. Incredible!

When I bought R&J Health Studio, I inherited a lot of members from the previous owner. These members had been members of R & J Health Studio for many years. Legend has it that R&J was the oldest gym on the east coast. I remember one member, a great guy named "Old Man Arnie." In Brooklyn, everyone has a "name". We had "Big Scott", "Pretty boy Artie," "Boris the Russian", "Cathy with the abs", "Mouse", etc. Old Man Arnie was in great shape and was young and vibrant, even though the calendar said he was a senior citizen. One day, he came to me and said he wanted to put on some muscle. I suggested he "up" his protein and cut back on his training a little because he was training each body part too often. When you do that, it can inhibit muscle growth. Secretly, I thought he was too old to improve. A month or so later, he came to me excited that he had put on a few pounds of muscle. A couple of months after that, he had put on ten pounds of solid muscle. I have to say, he looked terrific. He is an inspiration to everyone who meets him. Like Jack LaLanne says, *"Workout or wear out."* Arnie choose to workout and in return he found the fountain of youth. Remember, the only way you hurt your body is by not using it! Oh yeah, old man Arnie told me that his wife was thrilled too!

MELT FAT AWAY WITH MUSCLE

Muscle burns fat! You don't have to look like Mr. or Ms. Olympia for this to be true. When you have more muscle on your body, your body requires more energy to operate, even at rest. So the bottom line is, your body will burn more calories during rest when you have more muscle. Workout and put muscle on and watch your body turn from a fat storage machine to a fat burning machine.

When I was younger, I could eat anything without gaining weight. As I got older, I started to put fat on. Then, my metabolism slowed down and I got even fatter. There were two reasons for this. When I was younger, I moved much more. Also, in those days, muscle was a larger percentage of my body mass. I was always doing something when I was younger – running, lifting weights, racket ball, swimming, roller skating, dancing. When that stopped, I wasn't as lean. As I aged, my hormonal structure changed and this affected my metabolism, which in turn, affected my fat vs. muscle mass. I had to change the way I was doing things. Eating cleaner and regular exercise helps with the hormonal decrease that we experience as we get older. *Don't grow old gracefully, fight it every step of the way!*

Lifting weights is not nuclear science. There are certain principles, yes, but it is not as complicated as some books and magazines make it out to be. Remember, people make money by marketing the new solution to your problem. Also remember, there are very few things that are new. Repackaged yes, but new? Not necessarily. Yes, we have technologies that are new, but our bodies work with the same principles that governed them some 3,000 years ago.

Resistance training is exactly like it sounds. You add resistance (weight) to your body and move it through a range of motion. When I work with someone showing them how to lift weights, I ask them to show me how their muscles move. For example, your biceps move your forearm from extended to contracted. Your chest moves your arms across your body, etc. When doing an exercise, just move your body in it's natural arc with added weight and you will be doing it effectively. Are there better ways to execute an exercise than others? Of course, there are. You will learn better ways as you go along. You will find one exercise more effective than another, but don't get hung up on that. The same is true in all sports. You must learn the basics first. Don't forget that all great athletes return to the basics, often. They are the most important elements of sports. It is said, that during practice, Michael Jordan was the first on the court, the last to leave and while on the court, he was practicing the basics. That is what allowed him to be so creative on game night. He didn't have to think about the basics. Work on the basics, and then you can get creative.

Your body grows when more demand is placed on it. Also, don't be surprised to find that your mind gets bored. Most experienced people switch their routines around to keep their work- outs fresh and exciting. I change mine every 30 days or sooner; and I recommend you do the same. I don't make a major change. I usually just change the rep range a little or the exercise choices for the body parts I work, on a certain day. *(Note: a" rep"or repetition is when an exercise has progressed through one complete range of motion and back to the beginning, i.e. lifting a weight up and down once.)* On a daily basis, I also mix-it-up. Every week's work-outs may have most of the same exercises in them, but I may change the order. I have been doing this for over 30 years and I like to change it up some. In the beginning, I stuck with the basics and didn't deviate.

MUSCLE ...IT'S FOR WOMEN ALSO

Yes, you heard me right! You women must concentrate on building muscle, also. You must stop focusing on losing weight and start focusing on building lean muscle. Throw your scale out the window, if you have to. Muscle is heavier than fat, so you might weigh more, but who cares, as long as you feel good, look good and are healthy. There is no reason why any woman should have weak hunched over shoulders due to weak muscles or flabby upper arms. Weight training is the prescription to these cosmetic concerns that can and will lead to devastating health problems.

OK, I can hear you right now, "But I don't want to look like a man!", "I don't want all those muscles". Don't worry about it; you won't look like a man. Women can't build muscle the way men can because they don't have testosterone like men do. In fact, most MEN don't even have the genetics to build huge muscles. I have said it before, muscle burns calories, even at rest. The problem is most women don't build enough muscle when they are young and then as they age they have a very fast decrease in the little muscle mass they DO have. This is a major health threat to women and leads to devastating health problems and needless, yet endless yo-yo dieting as women try to get their weight and health under control.

My wife has been working out with me for over two decades. She too was very concerned. She always said she didn't want to look like a football player. My wife is my training partner and works out exactly the same way I do. She does the same exercises, similar number of reps and sets. She doesn't lift the same weight as I do, but she does lift as heavy as she can. Men in the gym are always amazed at how strong she is, because she looks like a woman. She is 100% woman, not even an ounce of football player in my wife. She doesn't look like a football player or any other man, but she is in great shape. At an age when most women are falling apart, Cathy is getting better. In fact, women are always asking Cathy how she works out and why she works out with weights. She loves to tell them that she works out with weights for "anti-gravitational" reasons. Women everywhere are discovering the benefits of resistance training. Now it is your turn.

BE STRONG TO PERFORM

Years ago, the "authorities" used to say that lifting weights would make you "muscle bound". When I was in high school, my coach, Jim Fraley would have us lift weights. He is the same coach that coached the great Olympic discus thrower, Al Oerter and other Olympians. Even though he would have us lift, it was usually only on rain days or at best sporadically.

My whole perception of weight training changed when I went to Montreal with my family in 1976. My Mom and Dad got tickets to the Olympics. While there, I got to see Bruce Jenner stun the world and boy was he inspiring! I loved watching Bruce Jenner attack all ten of his events, but there was another athlete that really stood out in my mind all these years later.

Alberto Juantorena was the first athlete to ever win both the 400m and the 800m in the Olympics. He took gold medals at the 1976 Olympics in both of these events, but even more important to me was how he looked. That man looked like an anatomy chart. He was very strong and muscular. In fact, his nickname in his native Cuba is *El Caballo* (the horse). Boy, he looked like a thoroughbred. After seeing this incredible athlete, I went home and picked up the weights with a new vengeance and dedication. 30 years later, I still haven't put them down. In fact, I enjoy it more now then I did then. There is something cool about being in good shape as you get older. My children are getting older now and my boy's friend's dig it that I am in good shape. Now that both of my beautiful daughters are getting older, I like it that the boys that come around see a strong dad, instead of a couch potato. My girls may not dig it as much, but it does get my oldest daughter, Jessica, home on time. My youngest, Jacqueline, is only 12, so it isn't an issue with her just yet, thank goodness.

Action Steps

Remember, the world doesn't reward us for what we know;
it rewards us for what we do!

1. Incorporate regular activity into your day, take the stairs instead of the elevator or park a little farther away from the office or the shopping center.
2. Use it or lose it, use your muscles.
3. Muscle burns more calories than fat.
4. Women…. don't neglect your muscles.
5. The stronger you are, the better you will perform.

CHAPTER

$$\boxed{10}$$

Dramatically Transform Your Body into a Muscle Building, Fat Burning Dynamo

EXERCISES THAT WORK

Resistant training builds strength and size of the skeletal muscles. Research has shown that resistant training also builds bones. This gives you a more toned and energetic body.

I don't want you to waste a lot of time getting fancy. Yes, you can get very carried away with different exercises and machines, but if you want to get the best bang for your buck with regards to the quantity of time spent exercising vs. results gained, then stick with exercises that are proven to give you maximum results in a minimum amount of time. I am always amazed when I am in the gym and one of the personal trainers has an out-of-shape client sitting on an exercise ball, trying to lift weights at some weird angle, while kicking their leg out or doing some kind of oddball exercise. I have been doing this for 30 years and I don't do that kind of thing and most of the people that I know don't do it either. I always wonder how long they keep their clients. There is a time and a place for specialty training, but the best thing to do is to keep it simple and to get the best results in the least amount of time.

Good, basic, time tested exercises

For your legs: Squats, leg presses, leg extensions, lunges, leg curls and calf raises.

For your chest: Flat chest press, incline chest press, decline chest press, chest fly.

For your back: Chins, pull downs and rows.

For your shoulders: Shoulder press and lateral raises.

For your biceps: Curls

For your triceps: Press downs and triceps extensions.

For your abs: Crunches and/or leg raises.

The above are some basic exercises. Since these are some of the best, I suggest you learn these basics first. Then you can branch out and get fancy. Go to www. JohnMRowley.com/bookbonus to see how to do these exercises.

How to pick the right weight

When people first start working out with weights, they are concerned with whether they are using the correct weight, how many reps (short for repetition) they should do and how many sets of reps are they supposed to do for a given exercise Working in the 8 to 12 rep-range is best for muscle growth. When you use less than 8 reps, you are getting more into strength training. Once you go beyond past 12 reps, you are more into endurance, so I suggest you stick with the 8 to 12 rep-range.

When you get to the gym and pick up the weight for a given exercise and you can easily do 20 reps, you are lifting way too light. Add more weight until you can do more than 8 reps, but not more than 12 reps. When you get to the 12th rep, you should be struggling and unable to get the 13th rep. When you can do more than 12 reps with that weight, add more weight to that exercise. You will want to be able to do 8 reps and will stay at that heavier weight until you can easily complete 12 reps again. It is that simple. Now let's look at some training schedules that will give you great results.

Workout Schedules to fit all Schedules and Levels

There are endless ways to arrange your workout schedule. I know people that workout every other day. Some do it every day, others do two days on, one day off. The key is to design a routine that will work for you and your lifestyle. I personally like working out more often so I can get out of the gym a little faster and have plenty of energy to work each body part. If I am only doing one or two body parts a day, I can focus better.

Below, I have it broken up into beginner, intermediate and advanced. I would say a beginner would be someone who is totally inactive and has never worked out before or not for a very long time. An intermediate is someone who is a little active and has been training more than six months. Advanced is someone who has been training for more than a year and wants to go to an advanced level of muscularity and fitness. The key is to find a routine that works for you and stick to it. Quite honestly, I know people that are extremely advanced athletes, whose workout is similar to the beginner's workout but their intensity is very high. I know others that do the intermediate workout, but only do two days a week hitting each body part once a week with high intensity. As the intensity level of your workout rises, you will need to hit each body part less often in order to give it the rest it needs. When I was taking personal training clients, most of them would train with me three times per week for 30 minutes or less hitting each body part once per week. I have had some pretty advanced people that do this with me. The key is I train them very hard. All of them do cardio 3 to 6 days per week, depending on time restraints, diet and goals.

BEGINNER LEVEL

Aerobic Training

Twice a week do, twenty minutes of aerobic training, either first thing in the morning, immediately after your workout or on your non-weight training days.

Resistance Training

Do the prescribed workout two or three times a week, resting sixty to ninety seconds between each set.

Monday and Thursday or Monday, Wednesday and Friday

Squat	1 set of 10 – 12 reps
Lunge	1 set of 10 – 12 reps
Chest Press	1 set of 10 – 12 reps
Incline Chest Press	1 set of 10 – 12 reps
Pull Down	1 set of 10 – 12 reps
Row	1 set of 10 – 12 reps
Shoulder Press	1 set of 10 – 12 reps
Lateral Raise	1 set of 10 – 12 reps
Triceps Press Down	1 set of 10 – 12 reps
Curl	1 set of 10 – 12 reps
Crunch	1 set of 10 – 20 reps
Reverse Crunch	1 set of 10 – 20 reps

INTERMEDIATE LEVEL

Aerobic Training

Three to five times a week, do twenty to thirty minutes of aerobic training, either first thing in the morning, immediately after your workout or on your non-weight training days.

Resistance Training

Do the prescribed workout every other day, if you want to workout on the weekends. Or you can opt for Monday, Wednesday and Friday. Four days per week is popular by doing Monday, Tuesday, Thursday and Friday. All work well; it's just a matter of which you like best. Whichever plan you choose, just make sure you rest sixty to ninety seconds between each set. The workout below is described as Monday and Thursday and Tuesday and Friday, as well as "Day One" and "Day Two". If you are working out with weights every other day, just alternate between the "Day One" and "Day Two" workout.

Monday and Thursday (Day One)

Squat	2 - 3 sets of 10 – 12 reps
Leg Extension	2 - 3 sets of 10 – 12 reps
Leg Curl	2 - 3 sets of 10 – 12 reps
Standing Calf Raise	2 - 3 sets of 10 – 12 reps
Biceps Curl	2 - 3 sets of 10 – 12 reps
Seated Biceps Curl	2 - 3 sets of 10 – 12 reps
Triceps Press Down	2 - 3 sets of 10 – 12 reps
Lying Triceps Extension	2 - 3 sets of 10 – 12 reps
Crunch	2 – 3 sets of 10 – 20 reps
Reverse Crunch	2 – 3 sets of 10 – 20 reps

Tuesday and Friday (Day Two)

Chest Press	2 - 3 sets of 10 – 12 reps
Incline Chest Press	2 - 3 sets of 10 – 12 reps

Pull Down	2 - 3 sets of 10 – 12 reps
Cable Row	2 - 3 sets of 10 – 12 reps
Shoulder Press	2 - 3 sets of 10 – 12 reps
Lateral Raise	2 - 3 sets of 10 – 12 reps
Crunch	2 – 3 sets of 10 – 20 reps
Reverse Crunch	2 – 3 sets of 10 – 20 reps

ADVANCED LEVEL

Aerobic Training

Four to six times a week do, thirty to forty five minutes of aerobic training, either first thing in the morning or immediately after your work-out.

Resistance Training

Choose one of the prescribed workouts depending on what appeals to you and what works for your schedule. Keep in mind, the more often you are in the gym, the shorter your exercise routine will be. No matter what, rest sixty to ninety seconds between each set.

WORKOUT 1

Mondays (Chest, Biceps and Abs.)

Chest Press	3 sets of 8 – 12 reps
Incline Chest Press	3 sets of 8 – 12 reps
Decline Chest Press	3 sets of 8 – 12 reps
Biceps Curl	3 sets of 8 – 12 reps

Preacher Curl	3 sets of 8 – 12 reps
Crunch	3 sets of 10 – 20+ reps
Reverse Crunch	3 sets of 10 – 20+ reps

Tuesday (Legs and Abs.)

Leg Extension	3 sets of 8 – 12 reps
Leg Press or Squat	3 sets of 8 – 12 reps
Lunge	3 sets of 8 – 12 reps
Hamstring Curl	3 sets of 8 – 12 reps
Standing Calf Raise	3 sets of 8 – 12 reps
Crunch	3 sets of 10 – 20+ reps
Reverse Crunch	3 sets of 10 – 20+ reps

Thursday (Shoulders, Triceps and Abs.)

Shoulder Press	3 sets of 8 – 12 reps
Lateral Raise	3 sets of 8 – 12 reps
Rear Delt Machine	3 sets of 8 – 12 reps
Triceps Press Down	3 sets of 8 – 12 reps
Lying Triceps Extension	3 sets of 8 – 12 reps
Crunch	3 sets of 10 – 20+ reps
Reverse Crunch	3 sets of 10 – 20+ reps

Friday (Back and Abs.)

Pulldowns or Chins	3 sets of 8 – 12 reps
Close Grip Pull downs	3 sets of 8 – 12 reps
Low Cable Row	3 sets of 8 – 12 reps

High Hammer Row	3 sets of 8 – 12 reps
Hyper Extensions	3 sets of 10 – 20 reps
Crunch	3 sets of 10 – 20+ reps
Reverse Crunch	3 sets of 10 – 20+ reps

WORKOUT 2

Mondays (Chest and Abs.)

Chest Press	3 sets of 8 – 12 reps
Incline Chest Press	3 sets of 8 – 12 reps
Decline Chest Press	3 sets of 8 – 12 reps
Cable Crossovers	3 sets of 8 – 12 reps
Crunch	3 sets of 10 – 20+ reps
Reverse Crunch	3 sets of 10 – 20+ reps

Tuesday (Legs and Abs.)

Leg Extension	3 sets of 8 – 12 reps
Leg Press or Squat	3 sets of 8 – 12 reps
Lunge	3 sets of 8 – 12 reps
Hamstring Curl	3 sets of 8 – 12 reps
Standing Calf Raise	3 sets of 8 – 12 reps
Crunch	3 sets of 10 – 20+ reps
Reverse Crunch	3 sets of 10 – 20+ reps

Wednesday (Back and Abs.)

Pulldowns or Chins	3 sets of 8 – 12 reps
Close Grip Pull downs	3 sets of 8 – 12 reps

Low Cable Row	3 sets of 8 – 12 reps
High Hammer Row	3 sets of 8 – 12 reps
Hyper Extensions	3 sets of 10 – 20 reps
Crunch	3 sets of 10 – 20+ reps
Reverse Crunch	3 sets of 10 – 20+ reps

Thursday (Shoulders and Abs.)

Dumbbell Shoulder Press	3 sets of 8 – 12 reps
Lateral Raise	3 sets of 8 – 12 reps
Hammer Shoulder Press	2 sets of 8 – 12 reps
Rear Delt Machine	3 sets of 8 – 12 reps
Crunch	3 sets of 10 – 20+ reps
Reverse Crunch	3 sets of 10 – 20+ reps

Friday (Arms and Abs.)

Biceps Curl	3 sets of 8 – 12 reps
Seated Biceps Curl	2 sets of 8 – 12 reps
Preacher Curl	2 sets of 8 – 12 reps
Triceps Press downs	3 sets of 8 – 12 reps
Lying Triceps Extension	2 sets of 10 – 20 reps
Dips	2 sets of 10 – 20 reps
Crunch	3 sets of 10 – 20+ reps
Reverse Crunch	3 sets of 10 – 20+ reps

WORKOUT 3 *(Only have three days a week to work out)*

Mondays (Chest, Shoulder, Triceps and Abs.)

| Chest Press | 3 sets of 8 – 12 reps |

Incline Chest Press	3 sets of 8 – 12 reps
Shoulder Press	3 sets of 8 – 12 reps
Lateral Raise	3 sets of 8 – 12 reps
Triceps Press Down	3 sets of 8 – 12 reps
Lying Triceps Extension	3 sets of 8 – 12 reps
Crunch	3 sets of 10 – 20+ reps
Reverse Crunch	3 sets of 10 – 20+ reps

Wednesday (Legs and Abs.)

Leg Extension	3 sets of 10 – 20 reps
Leg Press	3 sets of 10 – 20 reps
Lunges	3 sets of 10 – 20 reps
Leg Curls	3 sets of 10 – 20 reps
Standing Calf Raises	3 sets of 10 – 20 reps
Seated Calf Raises	3 sets of 10 – 20 reps
Crunch	3 sets of 10 – 20+ reps
Reverse Crunch	3 sets of 10 – 20+ reps

Friday (Back, Biceps and Abs.)

Pulldowns	3 sets of 10 – 20 reps
Close Grip Pulldowns	3 sets of 10 – 20 reps
Seated Rows	3 sets of 10 – 20 reps
Curls	3 sets of 10 – 20 reps
Preacher Curls	3 sets of 10 – 20 reps
Crunch	3 sets of 10 – 20+ reps
Reverse Crunch	3 sets of 10 – 20+ reps

The Power of Flexibility

Stretching

Staying flexible is very important. I often joke, that I better stay flexible, so I can "bend over backwards" to please my wife. The fact is, my wife has always "bent over backwards" to please me. Being flexible is very important and becomes more important as we age. Bob and Jean Anderson have a wonderful book called <u>Stretching</u> that I have used as a reference for many years. It is a no-nonsense book on stretching for a variety of purposes and I highly recommend it.

Staying flexible

Stretching keeps you flexible. But you must not over stretch too quickly, especially when you are not warmed up. I remember being in a fitness seminar over 20 years ago and the presenter took out a rubber band and rubbed it in his hands to make it warm and then, stretched it for all it was worth and it never broke. He then took the same rubber band and put it in ice water for a minute or so. He took the same rubber band out of the ice water and tried to stretch it again. This time, it didn't stretch too far before it snapped. The purpose of this demonstration was to illustrate that when your muscles are not warm and flexible, they will snap. I stretch after I do my cardio, but I also stretch the body part I am working on when I lift weights. While I am catching my breath between sets, I will just lightly stretch the muscle being worked. The key is just to stretch out and warm up a little first.

Action Steps

> *Remember, the world doesn't reward us for what we know;*
> *it rewards us for what we do!*

1. Find and join a gym.
2. Start learning how to do the exercises.
3. Experiment to find the right weight for each exercise.
4. Pick a routine that fits your schedule and one that you think you will enjoy.
5. Workout hard and smart.
6. Start looking for new clothes for your new body.

CHAPTER

$$\boxed{11}$$

Don't Neglect Cardio and Rest If You Want To Be Your Best!

The Third Leg: Aerobic Training

Be smart. Work you're heart

Your heart is magnificent. It takes oxygen rich blood and pumps it through your body. It then takes carbon dioxide laden blood back from the body and pumps it into the lungs, where it is expelled and exchanged for more oxygen.

Your heart starts beating before you are born and it doesn't stop until death. Ironically, the heart beats faster and less efficiently when you give it little to do, than when you put demands on it. They say that a boat will rust out much faster when sitting idle than when soaring the open seas. The same is true of an airplane. It will wear out quicker when sitting on the runway, than when flying through the heavens. The same is true with you. You must work your heart so it stays strong and healthy. One of the things I hear from a lot of people is, "I am going to take it easy tonight.", and "I am exhausted." Yes, they are working hard but they are exhausted because they are not feeding and utilizing their bodies properly. They are killing themselves by "taking it easy".

Cardiovascular Exercise

Cardiovascular exercise is a hotly debated topic among fitness experts. Some say that all you need is very brief, very intense bursts of cardio exercise done in an interval fashion and that will work your heart sufficiently. Then others say that you need to go long and slow. I believe that both are needed.

Let me explain. Short, intense interval training is a specific period of work, followed by another specific period of rest (i.e., 1 minute sprint followed by 2 minutes of walking). This is a great way to strengthen your heart and it helps with burning fat, but some of the best benefits with regards to burning fat are realized after the 20 minute mark. So the bottom line is, if you are trying to lose fat, try doing 30 to 45 minute sessions. If you can't, do what you can do, with the time that you have and build up the time.

Richard A. Winett has addressed this subject beautifully on his Master Trainer website (www.ageless-athletes.com). Richard starts off with an 8-minute graded warm-up, then goes into a 5-minute workout at 75% to 80% aerobic capacity, then does a 17-minute gradual cool down. Richard is a master of getting the most results from the least amount of time.

Heart rate

In the beginning, don't worry about putting your heart rate in the correct range. Just do something and progressively work up to getting your heart rate in the correct range. It is a good idea to monitor your heart rate, even in the beginning, to make sure it isn't too high and also to gauge how much more you can push yourself.

The formula that most people use for the heart rate is to take 220 minus your age and multiply it by how hard you want to work.

$$220 - 40 = 180$$
$$180 \times 70\% = 126$$

So according to this formula, if you were 40 years old, your maximum heart rate would be 180 beats per minute. If you wanted to be at 70% of capacity you would get your heart beat up to 126 beats per minute. The optimum zone is 55% to 85% of your maximum heart rate (MHR). Most machines now have heart rate monitors attached to the equipment or you can go to any sporting goods store and buy a heart rate monitor pretty inexpensively.

Here is a handy reference chart that you can use to find your ideal target heart rate. Simply look up your age and it will give you the target heart rate range that will work best for you. Like I said before, let's keep it simple.

Age	Target Heart Rate 55%	Target Heart Rate 85%

20 years	110 beats per minute	170 beats per minute
25 years	107 beats per minute	165 beats per minute
30 years	104 beats per minute	161 beats per minute
35 years	101 beats per minute	157 beats per minute
40 years	99 beats per minute	153 beats per minute
45 years	96 beats per minute	148 beats per minute
50 years	93 beats per minute	144 beats per minute
55 years	90 beats per minute	140 beats per minute
60 years	88 beats per minute	136 beats per minute
65 years	85 beats per minute	131 beats per minute
70 years	82 beats per minute	127 beats per minute
75 years	79 beats per minute	123 beats per minute
80 years	77 beats per minute	119 beats per minute
85 years	74 beats per minute	114 beats per minute
90 years	71 beats per minute	110 beats per minute

What type of Cardio?

The BEST type of cardio is the kind that you will actually do. So pick something that you enjoy. I like to ride my mountain bike with my wife and kids when I have the time. However, most of the time, I use my concept 2 rower, my Star Trac spinner or my Star Trac Pro recumbent bike at my home, because it is more convenient and I can do it consistently. My good friend John Guelzow works for Star Trac and gave me these pieces of equipment as a gift and it has made all the difference in the world. I usually do 30 to 45 minutes of cardio first thing in the morning with my wife. I like to switch it around so I don't get bored and it is also better on my joints to spread the stress around so we will usually do half of the time on one piece of equipment and half on the other.

Exercise doesn't have to be boring, just look for ways to stay active that fit into your lifestyle. Also, keep in mind that cardio is only good if you DO it; so, choose a time when you know you can do it. Of course, there is always the most effective time to do cardio. There are really two times that produce the best results. Doing cardio first thing in the morning, before you eat, works very well. Because your body has been fasting for eight hours or more, so when you are doing your cardio, your body will get to burning fat much faster than if you did it later in the day after you've been eating. Another very effective time is immediately after you've completed your weight training. The same principle applies, you burn your glycogen (blood sugar) when you are lifting weights and if you do your cardio immediately following, you will begin burning fat faster. The most important thing is to find a time that works best for you.

THE FOURTH LEG: REST & RECOVERY

Learn to relax. Your body is precious, as it houses your mind and spirit. Inner peace begins with a relaxed body. —NORMAN VINCENT PEALE

This sounds like a walk in the park, doesn't it? This fourth leg is no leg at all, you are thinking. WRONG!!! Rest too much and you will look and feel like it. Don't get enough rest and you will get over tired, chance getting hurt and you will not see the results of all the hard work you are putting into the other three legs. "Not fair!" you say. Too bad. This is the way God created you. Even God took a day off when He was creating the Universe. We need a day off from work to rest and recover.

Rest between sets

Resting between sets should last anywhere from 60 seconds to 3 minutes - sometimes even longer. It all depends on how heavy you are lifting and the type of exercise you are doing. For example, I may rest up to five minutes when doing heavy squats, but only 60 seconds when doing bicep curls. This amount of time allows the muscle to recover it's energy stores. Between sets, recovery will vary between individuals. Some people simply recover much faster than others, so pay attention to how you feel when you are working out.

Rest between workouts

Having your muscles fully recover before training them again is very important. What I am talking about is the recovery between training *sessions* of the same muscle group. Example: It should be the time between one chest workout until your next chest workout. It may be two days until your next chest workout or it may be a week.

This is very, very important for enhancing the muscle growth process. Most training programs have you training way too often. And ladies, I am talking to you too. Muscle growth will look like a tightening of your body parts, a sculpting, creating a new, younger, more shapely you. Ladies, you are NOT going to look like football players.

Muscles don't grow in the gym. Muscles grow when they are resting. Muscle must adapt to compensate for future stress by growing. Energy levels will fade, your appetite will suffer, and motivation will disappear, if you don't get enough rest. This is called over training.

On going rest and recovery

A good night's sleep is every bit as important as eating properly and exercising effectively. Statistics show that seven out of ten adults get six or fewer hours of sleep each night. Too many people think they can do without sleep. They are shooting themselves in the foot.

The average person is trying to get more done, so they spend more time doing things in place of sleep. They are exhausted all the time and can't focus properly because of fatigue, so it takes longer to do these things and then they must spend more time doing it. Do you see the problem here? It is a never ending loop.

You need more sleep in order to be energetic and productive. Most healthy adults need between seven and nine hours of sleep each night. Some need less and some need more but this is a good starting point. Find your cycle, stick to it and see how much your life changes. Your body lets you know when it is tired, so pay attention to it. If you don't, you will get irritable and have problems concentrating or remembering things.

GETTING A GOOD NIGHT'S SLEEP FOR A HIGH ENERGY DAY

With more activities than ever before pulling at you, you probably don't even realize how much your poor sleep habits are affecting your health, reducing your productivity, and lessening your enjoyment of life. If you're not well rested, all areas of your life will suffer. Your home life, work life, personal life and spiritual life are all affected when you don't get enough sleep.

First determine how much sleep you need. You probably have a rough idea of how many hours of sleep you need, so for a few days try to go to bed at a time that allows you that amount of sleep. Also pay attention and see if you get sleepy during the day. If you find yourself getting sleepier each day, you need more sleep than you thought. Give yourself extra sleep for a few days to try and find the right amount you need and soon your daytime alertness will reach a level you are happy with.   Once you know how much sleep you need, arrange your regular sleep schedule to give you that amount each night.   If you are a "morning person," like me, make sure you go to bed early enough to wake up rested. You may have to give up some social functions or stop watching some of your favorite TV shows. You will thank yourself for this as you find yourself with better health and more daily energy.

Tips for a Good Nights Sleep

- Avoid caffeinated drinks and alcohol in the evening.

- Don't eat large meals late at night. Your last meal of the day should be small and ideally, it should contain "slow" proteins (e.g., meats, cottage cheese or a casein drink which is just a milk-based protein drink you can get at most health food stores). This is so there will be a steady supply of amino acids into your bloodstream all night long, helping with muscle growth and fat loss.

- Try to go to bed at the same time most nights, with rare exceptions.

- Avoid upsetting yourself before bed…Don't watch the late news or review your overdue bills before going to bed.

- Unwind. Don't check E-mail or think about work related issues for at least an hour or two before bedtime.

- Develop and follow a bedtime ritual. For instance, take a bath or go for a light walk every night before going to bed. It will help you relax and get you ready for bed.

- Eliminate noise and outside light. Make sure that your bedroom is quiet the whole night and that you don't have a street light shining in on your face or that you have a Pit Bull puppy growling and protecting your whole house from under your bed, like we do.

- Keep the bedroom at a temperature that suits you. Most people sleep better when the room is a little cooler.

- Make sure your bed, mattress and pillows allow you to get a good night's sleep.

- Read something boring; usually you will be asleep within minutes.

- If you have an active mind and your thoughts are keeping you awake, try keeping a pad of paper next to your bed and write down everything in your head. This way you won't forget it and you can let go of it. I did this for many years with great results.

- Say your affirmations and be thankful for five things before you go to sleep.

Poor Sleep may make you Fat

According to <u>Reuters Health,</u> individuals who are overweight or obese report that they get less sleep per week than their normal weight counterparts. They further stated, that Dr. Robert D. Vorona and colleagues at Eastern Virginia Medical School in Norfolk, Virginia, interviewed 924 participants, ages 19 to 91 years, who completed questionnaires asking about medical problems and sleep habits.

Three factors affected total sleep time; being a night shift worker, being a male, and being obese, the team reported in the <u>Archives of Internal Medicine</u>. Vorona's group suggests, "Lost sleep may lead to metabolic and hormonal irregularities. For example, sleep restrictions may reduce levels of leptin, a hormone involved in appetite regulation, thus encouraging weight gain. Or it may simply be related to increased eating during increased time awake." Either way, you should make sure you get enough sleep. Your body will thank you. All that to say...GET ENOUGH SLEEP!

Time for yourself

Many people tell me that they can't take a day off from work. I thoroughly disagree. I spent some years as a real estate broker, when I first moved to Raleigh, N.C. Most realtors work seven days a week and never take any time to themselves. I was committed to taking a day with my family for church and to spend time together. The funny thing was that I immediately realized increased sales. I was more rested, so I was better able to focus. All I can say is, I took the time off, I started to produce more and my income went up all while I was feeling stronger and more rested. End of story. This isn't complicated stuff here.

In order to have energy to fuel your passion, you have to take care of yourself. You learned how to strengthen your body so it will support your mind and spirit for lifelong success. We learned how to take care of your four legs of the fitness table, which are Nutrition, Resistance Training, Aerobic Training and Rest & Recovery. Do these things and not only will your energy soar, but you will look better and you will live a longer, more productive and rewarding life. Now, there ain't nothin' to it.....but to DO IT!

Action Steps

Remember, the world doesn't reward us for what we know;
it rewards us for what we do!

1. Pick a couple of cardio vascular exercises that you would like to do.
2. Set a start date of when you will start exercising, no more than a week down the road.
3. Write down three things that are not enhancing your life that you could give up, making time for your new exercise routine.
4. Pre-schedule the time you will go to bed and stick with it.
5. Set the alarm for the time you want to get up and get on a schedule.
6. Make sure you have enough time between workouts so you can recover properly.
7. Have time for yourself set aside so you can recharge. Try taking every Sunday off and spend it with your family.

Lifestyle... The Blue Print (Designing an Energetic Successful Life)

CONQUERING THE TIME BANDIT

Have you noticed that time management and time management tools such as day timers, computer personal management programs, PDA's, date books on your cell phones and paper based systems, books, tapes and seminars on time management, etc have turned into a multi- million dollar business? This is because everyone feels like they don't have enough time to get everything done. It doesn't matter if you are a student, business person, stay at home mom, entrepreneur or employee. No one has enough time today.

Throw your day timer away because that is not the problem! Right now. Just toss it in the trash can and never look back. OK. Now that I have your attention, take your day timer out of the garbage. Brush it off and realize that tossing it in the trash is not the answer and you can use it to schedule your time. It is an effective tool, but not the answer to the true problem. The problem is not time. The problem is this, not having enough energy to use your time properly. Yes, you read that correctly. Unfortunately, the time management industry, and quite honestly, we have used this as an excuse for not living up to our expectations. Time management or lack there of, has turned into an excuse in the business world the same way carbohydrates have turned into the bad guy and excuse in the diet industry.

Very few people actually say they are too tired to live with passion. They blame it on the bandit....*time.* They simply don't have enough *time* to do everything. **Sure** they don't have enough *time.* They are unfocused and drag through the day, taking too long to do tasks because of their lack of focus. Then, when they go home to sleep they have an un-restful night's sleep and wake up tired. This is an endless, but unnecessary, cycle for many today. We are all given the same 10,080 minutes in a week. Some people have the time to change the world and some barely have the time to change their socks. Time isn't the issue. *The real issue is having enough energy to use the time given to us effectively.* Think about that for a moment. It is very profound, if I do say so myself.

INCORPORATING FITNESS INTO YOUR LIFE

I am dying with the help of too many physicians.
—ALEXANDER THE GREAT (356 BC – 323 BC),
A SELF-DIAGNOSIS ON HIS DEATHBED: 13 JUNE 323 BC.

Planning and Scheduling

Your health and fitness is your responsibility, not the doctor's. The doctor's job is to help you when you are already sick. Your job is to not get sick. In fact, some of my personal training clients are doctors and they know little about diet and exercise and they are quick to admit it. Planning your time is the key to great health and fitness, as well as success in all areas of your life.

As I said before, everyone has the same 10,080 minutes in a week. It is just that some use it better than others. Look at it this way, everyone has the same amount of time, so success in life is not about having more time but how you use the time you are given. So the excuse that you don't have enough time to eat right or exercise will not exist once you finish reading this. You do have enough time if you commit to a lifestyle that supports you instead of cripples you.

Time Blocking

There are many ways to schedule your time but the easiest and most effective way I have found is called time blocking. This can be done in many ways. You can block off whole days for certain aspects of your life or you can break each day down into blocks of time. I choose the latter because I find it more effective for me.

First, define the most important things that you need to get done. Then put them into time blocks. What this does is allow you to put the most important things into your schedule and make that time non-negotiable. You schedule the appropriate time to get things done. Everything else gets scheduled around these "must do" items. You have an appointment with yourself, so you don't miss it.

Below is an example of how you may block off your day.

MONDAY	
TIME	
6:00 – 7:00 AM	Cardio
7:00 – 9:00 AM	Prepare for and travel to work
9:00 – 11:00 AM	Paper work
11:00 – 12:00 PM	
12:00 – 1:30 PM	Lunch meeting
1:30 – 3:00 PM	Return phone calls
3:00 – 4:00 PM	
4:00 – 5:00 PM	Prepare for tomorrow's phone conference
5:30 – 6:30 PM	Gym (chest, biceps & abs)
7:00 PM	Home
NOTE: You don't' need to schedule every minute, this is just an example. Some people schedule their meals, as well. Some use more time blocks, some use less.	

Below is an example of a simpler one, like the one I use. As anyone who knows me can attest to, I don't like a lot of structure. I ALWAYS "hard" schedule the things that are important.

MONDAY	
TIME	
5:00 – 6:00 AM	Cardio
8:00 – 11:30 AM	Office

2:00 – 4:00 PM	Out of office appointments
5:30 – 6:30 PM	Gym (chest, biceps & abs)
NOTE: This just structures your day with the important details and then you fill in the rest of your schedule as needed.	

My wife Cathy and I do our cardio workouts first thing in the morning and this works for us. In fact, for years we did our whole workout at that time. But, due to our changing lifestyle and that of our children, we recently have started to lift weights in the late morning before lunch. This is our "lunch break". We have a schedule that works for us and supports our lifestyle. Cathy sets up the coffee pot the night before and puts it on auto timer. Cathy has more energy at night than I do. Then in the morning, I get up at very early, jump out of bed and pour us our coffee and I serve Cathy her coffee in bed. This works for us and we have been doing it for most of our 24 years of marriage. She loves being served her coffee in bed, it makes her feel loved even though she doesn't feel like getting up that early. And I love having the coffee ready, so all I have to do is pour it. Cathy and I have busy lives with lots of demands, this gives us time in the morning together where we can talk and spend some time together. Find out what works for you.

We have four incredible children, a beautiful daughter-in-law, a precious granddaughter, four energetic dogs and varied business responsibilities. If we did not make time for ourselves to workout, we would never be able to FIND the time to workout. We are committed to taking care of our bodies so we can live a passion-filled and energetic life.

My friend, Mitch Mayer, lives in South Hampton on Long Island and he does his workout at the end of the day. He is 54 years old and in incredible shape. Mitch and I used to train together when we worked together in Manhattan real estate and we compromised. For a few years, when my children where young, Mitch and I would train at lunch time. But as soon as we stopped training together I went back to 5:00 AM and Mitch went back to his evening workout. Each of us went to our natural comfort level as far as planning our individual workout time. You must find a time that works for you and stick to it. Don't worry about your energy levels, your body will get used to it in a few days. If I have to switch to an afternoon or an evening workout, I am exhausted. The funny thing is that when I switched from my lunch time workouts with Mitch back to my 5:00 AM workouts, I was exhausted at 5:00 AM for a few weeks. Your body will adapt and get used to the time you decide on. The key is to be consistent and to schedule it. In ink!

RELAX AND GET MORE ENERGY

The average American has forgotten how to relax. In fact, the average American has a hard time sleeping. The sleeping pill business has turned into a multi-billion dollar business with close to 25% of Americans taking them. Unfortunately, many that are not taking sleeping pills to get to sleep need a couple of drinks to unwind or the stealth drug of choice for many Americans...FOOD. The pressures of trying to juggle the increased demands of business, along with family life and other obligations is turning us into an exhausted society that has forgotten how to relax. We need to learn how to relax our body, mind and spirit on a regular basis, so we can be more productive and live more enjoyable lives.

When I was a young man working for my father, another of his employees was "Pops". That is what everyone called him. Pops was a great old southern man who had moved north for a better life. I worked with him in a New York City public school and spent many summers and holidays learning from him. One day, I was running around doing my work in a frantic way and he scolded me, "You burn up so much energy frettin'and fussin', that you wear yourself out and have nothin' left. Now, if you just chilled out a little, and moseyed instead of runnin' all the time, you would have more energy and you would get just as much work done, maybe even more. Plus, you would get to enjoy your life instead of tryin' to rush through it."

Pops knew I was a runner, so he asked me, "When you run, do you try to relax or do you force it"? I told him, "Of course, I relax. Because if I force it I will "tie up and die". All of my muscles will get tight and I will slow down". Old Pops just smiled his wry grin and said "Yep. Then why would life be any different? Relax and get more done". Now Pops was a master of being able to relax. One time, we were all playing cards in the men's locker room and old Pops just fell asleep in the middle of the game with a cigarette in his hand. I went to wake him up and the other men stopped me. They said, "Johnny boy, he does this all the time. When the cigarette burns down low enough, it will wake him…real quick!" And they all quietly chuckled. It was one of the funniest things I had ever seen. Ol' Pops being woken up by the burn was funny, but the howling laughter from the men and then from Pops was absolutely hysterical. This was a great group of guys, they knew how to work hard, play hard and relax hard. It was a great lesson for me.

Plug the dam on your energy leaks

Self-mastery and self-improvement are an ongoing process. In order to plug your energy leaks, first start off by giving yourself a break. We all have to start somewhere, so be okay with wherever you are starting. It is okay to be you. In fact, it is incredible to be you. No other you was or ever will be created, so be the best you, you can be. You are a gift to the world! We need you. There is something in you that we all need. What are YOU gifted at? Have you ever noticed at Christmas time or for a birthday, the joy and excitement that comes with opening the gifts? Well, you should have that same excitement with your life because you are the gift and the world is waiting for you with joy and excitement.

If you noticed, I began this book with motivational and self mastery techniques. The reason for that is because it is proven that what happens on the inside will greatly affect what happens on the outside. What you put in your head is as important as what goes in your mouth. It all works together. You have to eat and exercise effectively, plan your time, set your goals, change your self-defeating habits, model the success of others AND attack life with vim and vigor. Then you will have a full life, the life of your dreams, the life you where created for.

The No Exception Rule

The "No Exceptions Rule" is one that I learned the hard way. I have read in books to take an off-day and to cheat on my diet. I know myself well, so I never do that. A few years ago, I had just lost 20 lbs. of fat and I looked great. We went to visit my sister-in-law in Alabama for Thanksgiving. I was very careful with my diet for the first day or so there, and then it happened. My niece made a cheese cake. To say it didn't look right would be an understatement. She was upset and all the other kids where having fun teasing her. I wanted to ease her pain, so I made a fuss over how good it looked, and then she said do you want some Uncle John? Did I mention before that I can handle anything, except temptation? Now, I am a good guy, so I took a small piece of the cheese cake so my niece would feel good. I made the exception and it tasted so good. Well, to make a long story longer, I ate that whole cake, part of another and did not stop eating for a year. I put on the 20 lbs that I lost and an additional 10 lbs. I never should have made that exception during that part of my life, because I knew myself. Back then, for some reason, I would make the "exception" day by day and promise myself I would start eating properly the next day, unfortunately, the next day didn't come for a whole year. Now I can indulge, occasionally.

Keep in mind that we don't get fat, go broke or ruin relationships by the things we do once in a while. It is what we do consistently that counts. As Zig Ziglar says, "Failure is an event not a person." But failures add up; the failure to not make the call, the failure to not eat properly, the failure to not say, "I love you" to your spouse and children, the failure to not go the gym. These failures stack up on top of each other and over time they become overwhelming. If you have a drinking problem, don't ever take the first drink. The exceptions will become the rule, not the exception. So on the things that you know are difficult for you, don't make the exception.

EATING OUT

Eating out is a challenge for everyone. I am going to tell you what I do and what a lot of other people that I know do. Being fit doesn't mean that you have to stop going to restaurants and eating out. In fact, you should be able to enjoy eating out and staying fit and staying healthy. Of course, you will learn which restaurants are friendly to your goals and which ones aren't.

My wife and I eat out often. Many times we are in a hurry during business hours and want to meet for a quick lunch, so this is what we do. We have a couple of places we go to for lunch that work with us. First, we have a favorite Mexican restaurant that we go to often. We will ask them to grill us up a couple of chicken breasts with the Mexican seasoning and just put them on a bed of tomatoes and lettuce along with a glass of water with lemon. I also ask them to take the chips off of the table because if they stay there, I will eat them, all of them and then ask for another basketful. When we are in a real hurry, we will go to Subway or another sandwich shop and ask for turkey or some lean protein on a salad. Most sandwich places now serve salads. Chinese food is another good option. I get steamed veggies and chicken most of the time and sometimes splurge and get steamed shrimp. If I am in a wild mood, I will get shrimp and chicken together with my steamed veggies and I always ask and pay for extra chicken. I also like Ted's Montana Grill. Ted Turner has done a wonderful job with this restaurant. The food and the atmosphere are wonderful. What I like is the fact that I can get buffalo cooked many different ways and it tastes incredible. The buffalo meat or bison is very low in fat and very high in protein and tastes great in a burger or a steak. Again, I will eat the meat, veggies and no bread.

John and Cathy with Lou and Carla Ferrigno

Most restaurants are willing to accommodate your needs if you can specifically tell them what you want. One day, my family and I joined the Ferrigno family for dinner at the Fashion Café in Manhattan. Lou, his wife Carla and their children are a wonderful family and fun to be with. When we went to dinner, the waitress knew that Lou would eat a lot just by looking at him, so they accommodated him without his ever asking. Everything Lou ate was clean and healthy, but the serving sizes where superhuman. When our salads came, we all got regular sized salad bowls except Lou. They gave him a bowl the size you would use to feed a large family at Thanksgiving dinner. I thought it was hysterical. Even though Lou ate quite a bit, everything he ate was healthy. If you ever see Lou, you will know that he takes his fitness very seriously. He looks absolutely incredible…no pun intended. He is a wonderful example of how the fitness lifestyle can keep you young and vibrant as you age.

DINNER PARTIES AND GATHERINGS

I truly believe that getting together with other like-minded people is as important to a person as water is to a fish. Fellowship and friendship is definitely enhancing to our lives. I also believe that the dinner party, covered dish, pot-luck or whatever you call it is flawed at best. Ok, ok hold on don't throw this book at the wall just yet. Keep reading. Think about it for a minute. You get together with your friends and you eat cakes, pies, fried chicken, pig, etc. I did this also for a while and I got fatter every year. I started getting active in my church and they had what they call covered dish dinners. This is where every person brings a dish and shares it with everyone else. It is a wonderful concept, but what I found was that the longer I did this the fatter I was getting. I am not criticizing these people, they are all wonderful. But I was supposed to be an athlete! I still went to the gym, but my energy went into the toilet. I was tired, irritable and getting fat. We are sent here to contribute to the world and I kept finding myself more tired and irritable. Who could I help when I was feeling so lousy myself? Well, I could only help few people, because I was exhausted. I couldn't contribute at the level I wanted to because I was poisoning myself with the most available drug of all…food!

The fact of the matter is, we need to get together but we also need to eat right, especially when we gather. It is easier to eat right in groups, because we can hold each other accountable. That is why so many organizations have accountability and support groups because tough things are easier to deal with when supported by others. In fact, I get together with two other men the first and third Wednesday of each month for a time of accountability, prayer and a few laughs. But I think we need to redeem our time together. Let's take the get-together and turn it into something where everyone leaves spiritually and physically healthier. When we gather together let's bring fruit, vegetables, salads, whole grains and lean meats to eat, with water to drink, like you are learning to do in this book. Go back to the world stronger physically and spiritually. Then watch what happens. You will become someone others will aspire to be like.

FOOD AROUND THE HOUSE

If you have the right food around the house, it is easier to eat tasty things that are healthier for you. I have four children. I know it is hard when you have snack foods around the house. I told you before that I ask my kids to hide the snack foods and they are glad to do so because they know if they don't hide them, I will eat their snacks and there will be no more for them, or worse, I will throw their snacks away so I am not tempted. Plus, they make a game out of it. There are some very healthy alternatives to some of your favorite unhealthy foods.

Here is an example of my shopping list:

- Fresh and frozen chicken breast
- Fresh and frozen turkey breast
- Canned tuna
- Fresh tuna
- Ground turkey or chicken breast (Be careful to look at the cholesterol content. Lately, the food industry has more cholesterol in some brands of ground turkey than you'll find in deli meat or hamburger.)
- Eggs and egg whites in a box
- Steel cut oats
- Oat groats
- Rye
- Metamucil
- Cottage cheese
- Frozen mixed veggies and frozen broccoli
- Fresh vegetables

- Fresh fruit
- Frozen fruit (for protein drinks)
- Canned pineapples (in its own juice)
- Spelt pasta (spelt is an excellent wheat alternative, many have allergies to wheat)
- Spelt bread
- Skim milk
- Sparkling water
- Sugar free, fat-free pudding mix (mix with protein powder for a great snack)
- Green tea
- Protein powder
- Lemon juice (I put this in my water)

WHEN SHOULD I EAT AND HOW OFTEN?

Put yourself on a schedule to eat a small meal or have a healthy snack a total of six times a day. It isn't hard. Once your metabolism resets itself, you will start to feel hungry when you don't eat at these times. The best time to eat is when you are hungry and if possible before you even get hungry. Let me elaborate. You need to eat before you get too hungry, so you don't binge. If I don't eat when I need to, then my blood sugar drops too low and all I want to eat are snacks. Also, you need to eat first thing in the morning, You need to feed your body after an 8 to 10 hour fast. Now don't tell me that first thing in the morning you are not hungry. Eat anyway, or you need to at least have a protein drink. This will serve two purposes. First, it will feed your body. Second, it will keep your blood sugars level.

Sometimes when I go to church, I bring a protein drink with me or I eat right before I go. Sometimes I do both. I have to or I get hungry and you know what THAT means. The service at my church can last a couple of hours. By the time we talk to everyone, it may even be 3 hours before we can leave and have lunch. If I don't eat, I will be so hungry when we do finally eat, that I will just dig into anything. Instead, the protein drink keeps my blood sugar at an even keel and I am fine when we go out to eat.

One Sunday, Bill Kazmaier was in town and went out to eat with my wife, Cathy, our friend, John Guelzow and myself. Bill is the strongest man in the world and does he look it. He is one of the largest men I have ever seen. The only thing more impressive than his body is his heart. What a great guy! He came all the way to Raleigh to speak at a couple of YMCA's, a local gym, and at my church, all to help people. He also did this for no fee. I got to see up close how he keeps his huge, muscular physique. That man can eat! Boy, when we went out it was like an eating contest. The one thing that I noticed was that we all were eating a lot of steak, chicken, turkey, vegetables and fruit. We were at a local restaurant, which has an all-you-can-eat buffet on Sundays. We sure got our money's worth, and we felt great when we left, full but energetic. On the flip side of this, when we go out with other people, everyone is eating bread, pasta, stuffing and cakes; everyone leaves exhausted. You can eat a lot if you are eating the right things.

BE PREPARED TO EAT SO YOU CAN EAT OFTEN

When I worked in Manhattan, I would get to my office at 7:00 AM. I would not eat any breakfast before leaving because I was not hungry and I was always in a hurry to get to the office early. I started to get a bagel and coffee for breakfast, then at around 9:00 AM or 10:00 AM the coffee cart would come around and I would have something else quick to eat and wash that down with another cup of coffee. Then at 12:00 PM, it was off to the Post House or Sparks for lunch and since I wasn't eating well, I was starving and would eat one or two baskets of bread before my lunch would arrive. I blew up like a house. I got fat, my dress shirts didn't fit anymore and I felt lousy. I was losing the very edge that made me successful in the toughest real estate market in the world. I was losing my energy and my enthusiasm.

Thank goodness this didn't last too long. I went out and bought a blender and a small refrigerator for my office. I would have a meal replacement or a protein drink first thing in the morning and then another one around 10:00 AM. I would also keep fruit and bring in leftover chicken and brown rice that I made at home in my steamer. I would simply put chicken and rice in a zip lock bag and bring it with me. I got this zip lock bag trick from some of the professional body builders that I had become friends with. They will cook all of their food for four days in advance, store it in the refrigerator divided into gallon size zip-lock bags and carry it around with them.

Ray Stern, a professional wrestler and dear friend, who made it big in real estate developing and in the airline business, would bring a whole cooler full of chickens when he traveled. He would have his chef cook them and load them in a cooler. Ray is in his 70's, I believe, and in great shape (Ray is in such good shape it is hard to tell how old he really is). Ray started working out at the gym that I owned, long before I owned it. He has used his fitness in a powerful way during his life. He has a wonderful book out called the Power of Thunder. It is definitely worth a read.

I always loved it when Ray came by my gym. One time he popped in and he was wearing his trademark Rolex. This Rolex watch is incredible, very large with diamonds all over it. Ray was talking with me by the front desk and a few tough kids from the neighborhood came in. Ray cheerfully said, "Hello", but as the guys walked past, one of the guys said, "I bet we could take that watch from him." Well Ray never wanting to pass up a challenge said, "Okay, let's see if ALL of you guys can take it from me. If you can, it's yours." He said this with a great big smile. (One thing these guys didn't know was that Ray is famous for wrestling alligators and bears...and winning.) Well, these guys backed down and Ray had a good laugh. Ray is in great shape, strong, vibrant and a lot of fun to be around. He is a wonderful example of using an energetic and healthy body to excel in life.

SPIRITUAL SANDPAPER

Regardless of how much we try to live a fit and energetic lifestyle there is always going to be that person or persons who want to see you frustrated and fail. Do you have the "special person" or persons in your life who just bug the heck out of you? No matter how hard you try, they just get under your skin. You don't want to be around them, no less speak to them, but you have to, because you work for them or work with them or you married into their family or they are in your own family. Well, we all have these special people in our lives and they are there for a reason. They are "spiritual sandpaper"!

Just take a moment to just think about this person in your life, and then reflect on the fact that they may be in your life for a purpose. Does it make you feel any better that they may be there for a divine reason? No? Well, me neither. It doesn't make me feel a bit more joyful about this person, being in my life and having to deal with them, when they just drive me bonkers. Until... I see the fruit of the relationship. Sometimes, the fruit is the way I have grown through dealing with this person and sometimes the fruit is the way the other person has grown and changed. So, now when I deal with my "spiritual sandpaper", I have a little private chuckle. When I see this person heading my way, I quietly and sarcastically give thanks for this person and once I get this chuckle out of the way, I really am thankful because of what is coming out of it.

Sandpaper has its place. I own a painting company. It's a well known and respected one in our community. We finish multi-million dollar homes in exclusive communities and sandpaper is a tremendous tool. It takes off the rough edges so we can bring the surface to a fine finish. This person is in your life, so the rough edges come off of you. So you can be brought to a fine finish. Just realizing this will help you cope much more effectively with these select "special" people in your life. Oh, I have to run, my phone is ringing and it is my "spiritual sandpaper". My rough edges aren't completely off just yet. Or maybe the person calling has some rough edges that need some smoothing and I'm HIS sandpaper. Man, I hate the thought that I may be the "spiritual sandpaper" to this *"special"* person in my life. Don't forget, be kind to your "spiritual sandpaper" because more than likely, you are someone else's "spiritual sandpaper" and you may not even realize it.

The key is to put all these little obstacles in their proper place and live the lifestyle that supports you and your life.

THE POWER OF LIFESTYLE AND PEOPLE WHO LIVE IT!
REAL LIFE EXAMPLES

I want to just give you a few examples of people who are extremely busy and incorporate fitness into their lives in a way that supports them. I also want you to notice that they all workout a little differently, but their eating styles are similar.

1. **John & Cathy Rowley (47 years old & 43 years old)**

   - We workout with weights 4 to 6 times per week. We change our schedule during the year and usually use the two advanced workouts described in the exercise section of this book or something similar. We are in and out of the gym in less than 40 minutes.

   - We do some form of cardio 4 to 6 times per week, usually first thing in the morning.

   - We eat whole natural foods, our eating style is moderate in natural carbohydrates, low in fat (not too low), and high in good quality protein. Just like you are learning in this book.

   - We use protein shakes at least 3 times a day. We get a lot of our protein from protein supplements.

2. **Mitch Mayer (57 years old) (Retired real estate executive, retired teacher, now an active investor. He still works as a life guard in the summers at a Montauk point beach and his body is the envy of all the young lifeguards)**

   - Lifts weights 4 times per week. He lifts on Saturday, Sunday, Tuesday & Wednesday. He may have changed the days since retiring, so if you see an incredibly fit lifeguard at Montauk Point on Long Island, feel free to ask him what days he is working out.

- He works each body part once a week, but changes exercises and body part combinations every week. He does 3 or 4 exercises per body part. He does between 8 and 12 reps each exercise. His routines are like snow flakes, no two are the same. Mitch has been working out for many years and knows his body.

- Mitch eats whole natural foods, his eating style is high in natural carbohydrates, low in fat (not too low), with plenty of good quality protein. He tries to eat organic when possible.

- Mitch does 20 to 30 minutes of cardio after each workout.

- Mitch lives in South Hampton and soaks in the hot tub every night.

3. Clarence Bass (69 years old. Retired attorney, active fitness writer)
- Clarence works out twice a week.

- One day a week with weights and one day he does hard cardio.

- When he lifts weights he does a full body workout that lasts about 90 minutes. He works out very hard. I have tried his workout and it is brutal.

- His cardio is 20 minutes of intervals once a week.

- If you want his workout you can go to www.cbass.com and order one of his books. He has also offers plenty of free resources.

- He walks for an hour every evening.

- He eats three main meals a day and two snacks every day. His eating style is high in natural carbohydrates, moderate in fat with emphasis on "*good* fat." and includes plenty of good quality protein.

4. **Bob Bonham (55 years old, owner of *Strong and Shapely Gym* in East Rutherford, NJ)**

   - Works out with weights 4 to 6 times per week.

   His typical workout is:

   - Monday: Thighs and calves

   - Tuesday: Chest and biceps

   - Wednesday: Back, lower back and abs.

   - Thursday: Thighs and calves

   - Friday: Shoulders

   - Saturday: Arms

He varies his routine in sets and reps every 8 weeks going from the "old fashion" 20 reps on the first set to 4 - 6 reps on the last set. Bob says he trains just as hard as he did when he was younger, only smarter and as a result he carries more muscle. Late fall, he tends to ease up on his diet a little, but by late winter he tightens it up again and starts doing cardio.

5. Crystal Moore (40 years old, State Program Coordinator)

- Cardio 6x week (run 4x, cycle 2x for a minimum of 40 minutes per workout)

- Strength training 2x week for a minimum of 1 hour per workout. She trains the entire body in each session and uses medium weights and does three sets of each exercise and keeps her reps around 10 reps

- Always takes one day per week as her DDO - designated day off

Crystal says the key to her happiness is to eat a variety of foods in MODERATION. Because she runs, she can eat more carbs than she would if she didn't run. She balances her intake with low fat and an equal amount of protein and good carbs. Her daily caloric intake averages around 2400 calories. Her staples include fish, chicken and steamed vegetables. She snacks on bananas, energy bars and/or twigs and berries, (trail mix she makes herself comprised of dried fruits, nuts and seeds). She stays away from fried foods and bread. She also drinks a lot of water!

7. Leyla Akil (49 years old, she has 2 children; she is pursuing her Master's in teaching to make a career change. She works as a consultant and as a substitute teacher)

- Goes to the gym at least 4 days a week.

- She usually works on one body part (4 exercises, between 8 and 12 reps), except for legs which she break up into 2 separate days.

- After working on a body part, she likes to do between 20 – 45 minutes of either cardio or boxing. Boxing includes either hitting the speed bag or the heavy bag plus jumping rope. She also jogs outside at least 15 miles a week (which she loves).

- She is not very strict with her diet. She avoids junk food as much as possible and loves to eat fruits and vegetables.

- She doesn't believe in diets, but for as long as she can remember, she has been in the habit of eating small meals (maybe 4 or 5 a day) and snacks all day long. This, she believes has helped bless her with a fast metabolism which helps to keep her in shape.

As you can see, each of these people took different roads to the same destination. They have each maintained top physical condition, while holding demanding careers, having families and contributing to society. What they have in common is that they do the resistance training every week, they do some sort of cardio vascular exercise and they eat a lot of the right foods. That's it in a nut shell.

Although I struggled with this, I decided *against* putting pictures of these outstanding people in this book. I wanted to honor their hard work in this book, but more importantly, I want you to be the best "you", you can be. Sometimes comparing yourself to others is self-defeating. I have noticed that in many fitness books they have before and after pictures. I feel they are sometimes misleading and get the wrong message across. I know in my own personal quest, results have taken time and patience. I have never experienced instant results. Sylvester Stallone in his book, *"Sly Moves"* expresses this same message. This is what Sly said, *"Maybe it's just me, but in the first Rocky, I took supplements and worked out for six months, five hours a day, six days a week, and I never got a body like the one featured at the front of Bill's (Bill Phillip's "Body for Life") book — and I was under the watchful eye of boxing trainers and anxious studio executives. It took me from Rocky in 1975 until Rocky III in 1981 to get my "after" body."* No, it's not just you Sly, my experience has been the same. It takes time. Period! This book is about results, yes, but results that come out of a healthy lifestyle. This isn't a quick-fix book. It is a book on living a successful life empowered by a successful lifestyle.

CONCLUSION

Now you know how to go out and increase your energy, enhance the way you look, make yourself more vibrant, stronger and more confident. You have these things going for you so there is nothing you can't accomplish. The world needs your gifts; it is your responsibility to bring yourself to the world.

Action Steps

Remember, the world doesn't reward us for what we know;
it rewards us for what we do!

1. Schedule time for the things that are important.
2. Practice relaxing.
3. Learn what you can make exceptions on and what you can't.
4. Learn how to eat out and find restaurants that are friendly to your needs.
5. Keep good food around the house and make bad eating difficult.
6. Be prepared, so you can eat often.
7. Start to build fitness into your lifestyle.

CHAPTER

$$\boxed{13}$$

Recipes for Success

I would like to give you a few ideas to get your thoughts going. You can eat delicious food and still eat healthy. These are all quick to make and easy to prepare. Plus, they are tasty.

EGGS

Pumping Iron Breakfast

½ pound lean ground sirloin or lean ground turkey

1 small chopped onion

4 egg whites beaten

Fresh spinach leaves to taste chopped

Sea salt and ground pepper

In a large nonstick skillet, brown the meat along with the onions over a medium heat. Drain off excess fat. Add eggs, stirring constantly until firm. Spread spinach leaves over the top, cover, and remove from the heat. Let sit covered for 2 to 3 minutes to allow spinach to wilt. Add salt and pepper. Eat.

Basic Low-fat Omelet

4 to 6 egg whites beaten

Onion and mushrooms

1-2 slices of no fat cheese

In a large nonstick skillet sauté the onions and mushrooms. Stir in eggs and cook over a medium heat until firm. Put the fat-free cheese on the eggs and fold omelet in half. Cover and turn off heat. Let sit for 30 seconds to 1 minute to allow cheese to melt. Eat.

Oatmeal Pancakes

12 egg whites

1 cup of oatmeal

3 tablespoons of cinnamon

A little olive oil

Mix all the ingredients in a blender and then pour into a preheated non stick frying pan with a non stick spay. Cook until done.

Lunch

The Simple Sandwich

Whole wheat, whole grain or spelt bread

Low fat turkey

No-fat cheese

Lettuce

Tomato

Mustard

Put together and eat. Simple. You can do the same with any low-fat meat, left-over meats, tuna out of a can, etc. Easy and healthy.

Bison Burger

½ pound ground bison meat

No-fat cheese

Onion

Whole wheat, whole grain or spelt bun

In a non-stick skillet cook the ground bison into a patty. Once cooked, cover with the non-fat cheese and let cheese melt. You can put on the bun or have plain or over a bed of lettuce. You can add the onion sautéed or raw whatever you prefer. You can use lean ground turkey and lean ground beef for this, as well.

DINNER

Grilled or Broiled Chicken

Chicken breast

Fresh raw vegetables

Grill or broil the chicken and do the same with the vegetables. That is it, you have a great tasting, healthy dinner. You can do the same with fish or any good lean meat.

Steamed Chicken

Chicken breasts

Fresh raw vegetables

Low sodium soy sauce

Brown rice

Cook the brown rice according to the directions on the box. Put chopped chicken breast into a steamer and cook until done. During the last couple of minutes, add your vegetables to it. You can also add shrimp which makes for a delicious combination.

Put chicken and vegetable mixture over the brown rice and add a little low-sodium soy sauce and you have a delicious meal. Eat.

DESERT

High Protein Pudding

One packet of fat-free, sugar-free pudding

100 to 150 grams of whey protein powder

Soy milk or skim milk, add enough so it is the consistency you want. (what I like to do is use pasteurized egg whites from a container instead of the milk for an extra protein kick)

Combine the pudding and the whey protein in a mixing bowl. Add soy or skim milk until it is the consistency you like. Put in refrigerator for 10 minutes. You now have a healthy, high protein snack. When others break out the ice cream you bring out your high protein pudding.

Cottage Cheese and Pineapple

Low fat cottage cheese

Pineapple chunks

It is exactly what it sounds like. Add low fat cottage cheese to a bowl and top with pineapple. Cottage cheese has about 30 grams of protein per cup and is a great source of protein. Pineapple is succulent and refreshing! It is a winning combination.

AFTERWORD:

NOW IT IS YOUR TURN... TO CLIMB YOUR LADDER OF SUCCESS!

THIS ISN'T THE END, BUT just the beginning of your exciting journey! You now have the blueprints to build an energetic, strong, vibrant and healthy life. With just a few changes you can change the way you think, improve the way you eat, the way you exercise and in turn your whole life.

The principles, tips, tricks and techniques outlined throughout this book grow out of years of experience and research, and have definitely worked for me and for others who have applied them.

I close with these quotes:

The greatest achievements were at first and for a time dreams.
The oak sleeps in the acorn. —**JAMES ALLEN** (1864 – 1912), WRITER

You can't fly a kite unless you go against the wind and have a weight to keep it from turning somersaults. The same with man. No man will succeed unless he is ready to face and overcome difficulties and is prepared to assume responsibilities.
—WILLIAM J. H. BOETCKER

I am only one; but still I am one. I cannot do everything, but still I can do something. I will not refuse to do the something I can do.
—HELEN KELLER (1880 – 1968)

You lose with potential. You win with performance.
—BILL PARCELLS, PRO FOOTBALL COACH

Wherever you are, whatever your circumstances may be, whatever misfortune you may have suffered, the music of your life has not gone. It's inside you – if you listen to it, you can play it. — NIDO QUBEIN, PROFESSIONAL SPEAKER

Now go for your dreams with abandon, regardless of the obstacles that may litter your path. Those very obstacles may be unrealized opportunity. Do what you can do and start right where you are. Don't worry about what you think your potential is. Go out and do something. Start performing like a champ. Potential is useless, unless you do something. Go out and let your life's music play loud……. REAL LOUD . Let the world hear your song. The song of your life is a song of praise to your Creator. Don't just exist but really LIVE!

Do these things and I will see you on top of *YOUR ladder of success!*

BRING THE POWER OF TRANSFORMATION TO YOUR ORGANIZATION:
THE CLIMB YOUR LADDER OF SUCCESS™ WORKSHOP

A POSITIVE AND PROFOUND TRANSFORMATION is the result when your employees, managers, members and students experience *The Climb YOUR Ladder of Success* live group workshop.

The Climb YOUR Ladder of Success Workshop™ will empower them to be more productive with less effort. It will help them put more money in their pockets. They will function more effectively at work and discover they can now accomplish projects that are just sitting undone because they will have the energy and focus to get more done in the same amount of time. They will find they work better in groups and are more effective individually. It will help them to get more out of life and be more fulfilled.

The Climb YOUR Ladder of Success Workshop™ includes empowering tools to help with long term success. This workshop is ideal for groups such as:

- Sales professionals
- Business Owners
- Entrepreneurs
- Managers and executives
- Trade associations
- Corporate workgroups
- Students and educators
- School officials and administrators
- Military and civilian personnel
- Nonprofit groups
- Professional practitioners and their staff
- Employees facing downsizing or layoffs
- Government employees
- Multi level marketing sales professionals

TAKE YOUR QUEST FOR SUCCESS TO THE NEXT LEVEL...

Download Your **FREE BONUS GIFTS**

At **www.JohnMRowley.com/bookbonus**

As a purchaser of <u>*Climb YOUR Ladder of Success Without Running Out of Gas!*</u>, you're entitled to a special bonus from author John M. Rowley.

Now you can get the full video of how to perform each exercise discussed in this book. John will take you step by step through the execution of each exercise so you can achieve the most dynamic long-term results, in the least amount of time.

But that's not all!

John is making available to you for the first time all the forms that he uses in his live goal setting workshop so you can start creating a dynamic, passion filled life…NOW! You can go step by step through this life changing workshop and start setting and achieving your goals and start living a more empowered life immediately!

SIMPLY GO TO

www.JohnMRowley.com/bookbonus

TO GET STARTED TODAY!

ABOUT THE AUTHOR

JOHN M. ROWLEY'S AMAZING RISE to the top has become the stuff of legend and inspiration. His credentials include being a college athlete whose career was cut short by a near fatal car accident, a career as a janitor and the nerve to tackle the high powered world of Manhattan real estate and the dynamic international field of fitness. Although John's athletic career was cut short he studied kinesiology, exercise, anatomy, fitness and nutrition with intensity in order to get his body healthy again after the devastating accident.

Knowing success left clues, John also immersed himself in the study and implementation of the science of human potential and peak performance. Success came but not without obstacles. John has been on the verge of bankruptcy and at times his family didn't have food to eat or money to pay the bills but John was unwilling to give up. With his wife Cathy at his side and without connections John started at the bottom as a janitor in Brooklyn and then earned a position at one of the most prestigious real estate companies in Manhattan. John also bought R&J Health Studio, started several other companies and was involved with real estate investments over the years but John was always convinced that his savviest investment was in himself and in the people around him.

In real estate John made a name for himself managing some of the most prestigious properties on Park Avenue and the upper east side of New York and managing the holdings for many notables including Harry and Leona Helmsley. John also owned R&J Health Studio, the gym **known as "The East Coast Mecca of Bodybuilding." R&J Health Studio received international attention when it was featured in the movie, Pumping Iron, starring Arnold Schwarzenegger and Lou Ferrigno.** John is an internationally recognized motivational and fitness expert, and is a columnist for several publications and maintains an academic certification as a Certified Fitness Trainer. He routinely consults with athletes and business people alike helping them to revitalize their bodies and ignite their passion and energy through diet, exercise and a well balanced emotional and spiritual life for lifelong success.

John's motivational, inspirational and sometimes bold tell-it-like-it-is attitude is a fresh approach to lifelong success.

To find out more about John's workshops, training, books, and audio and video programs or to inquire about John's availability as a speaker or trainer, you can contact him at:

Rowley Results Unlimited

www.JohnMRowley.com

John@JohnMRowley.com